ALABAMA HISTORY IN THE U.S.

Angela Broyles

Bluewater Publications, U.S.A.

Bluewater Publications Killen, AL 35645 Bwpublications.com
Copyright 2003 © Angela Broyles & Bluewater Publications
First Edition

4th edition
© Copyright 2020 by Angela Broyles & Bluewater Publications
BWPublications.com
Killen, Alabama
Protected
Library of Congress Control Number: 2020933081
ISBN 978-1-949711-56-1

All rights reserved under International and Pan-American Copyright Convention. No part of this publication may be reproduced or transmitted in any form or by any means, electronic or mechanical, including photocopying, recording, or by any information storage and retrieval system, without prior written permission from the Publisher. Published in the United States by Bluewater Publications. This work is based from the author's personal research & interpretation.

Editor – Sandi Harvey
Interior Design - Maria Yasaka Beck

Published by:
Bluewater Publications
1812 CR 111
Killen, Alabama 35645
www.BWPublications.com

Acknowledgements

I want to express my heartfelt thanks to my dear husband Malcolm. Without Malcolm's love and support in raising our children I would never have acquired a love for history. Malcolm has been a great encourager of educational projects.

I would also like to thank Lee Freeman, Ronald Pettus and William Lindsay McDonald for their direction and encouragement. Their help has been invaluable. These three men are incredible researchers and historians who have given their life to preserving and teaching history to the next generations.

A special thanks to Susan Kirkman Vaughn for writing *Life in Alabama* & Elberta Taylor author of *Stories of Alabama*. We used portions of their out-of-print texts in this history course. Although these wonderful women are no longer physically living, their works live on in this publication and in the lives of those that read them.

Love to all on your educational journey,
Angela Broyles

How to Get the Best Results: A Note from the Author

Alabama History in the U.S. has been designed to be versatile making it user friendly for the student as well as educator. To get the best academic results using this study, there are some suggestions below. If you follow the suggestions you should have a full year history credit for students. As your students follow the suggested activities each should grow academically from the individual challenges. Each student should also gain an education in the following academic areas:

- Research Skills
- Writing
- Vocabulary
- Geography

Research Suggestions:

Research skills are even more important today than they were just ten years ago. These skills or the lack thereof can make a tremendous difference in the credibility of your writing. When you research, always cross-reference your findings to establish stronger credibility before you add to your paper. Of course, the younger student may not be ready for this level of research but it is important to begin introducing your student to this standard as early as possible. You may want to encourage your younger students in this area by taking them on a field trip to the genealogy department of your local library. Have the students help you find information.

There are several excellent sources for primary sources to acquire historical research. The local library's genealogy department is my favorite. Most people know very little about using the resources in the genealogy department. Please don't let that discourage you! I have visited genealogy departments all over the country, never having an unfriendly experience. The people you meet in the genealogy departments are most likely going to be thrilled that you are trying to learn. They will often walk you through the steps to locating the information you need.

Google Books has many primary sources digitized.

Vocabulary:

The vocabulary chosen is relative to the time period you will be studying. Student should write sentences using each word. If the student has trouble developing sentences, dictate sentences to them. You can slowly move the children from copying, to writing from dictation, to writing their own sentences.

History Journaling with the Timeline:
It's very important for the student to write daily about the things they have learned. The timeline journal gives them a place to engage in this activity and keep all the work in one location. The student will see progress more quickly if the writing is in one place. This activity also reinforces historical knowledge, giving the student not only the confidence and familiarity of writing their personal knowledge down; it's also an incredible exercise for building writing skills.

To print the PDF of the Alabama Timeline Journal, go to the website below.
tinyurl.com/alabamanotebook

Nature Studies:
Children can learn about nature and creation while just studying the habits of interesting animals. Leaf collections, labeling and adding notes about the leaves always add a lot to the study, we also try to always have sketches and/or pictures that would go with our study.

For animals, simply note what habitats they prefer, their reproductive process, what they eat, and if they are native to the state. You can add a picture or sketches that will give your nature study collection much more credibility.

Contents

CHAPTER 1: GEOGRAPHY 1
    Alabama the Heart of Dixie 4
    Alabama is a Good Place to Live 5
    The Mound Builders 5
    Building a Village 7

CHAPTER 2: DE SOTO & OTHER EXPLORERS 10
    Life in the Indian Village 13
    Indian Ways 14
    Juan Ortiz & the Arrival of the Spaniards 16
    Coming of the Spaniards 18
    De Soto and the Chief of Tuscaloosa 19
    Tuscaloosa 20

CHAPTER 3: FRENCH & ENGLISH 23
    Coming of the French 24
    Petticoat Rebellion 25
    The Building of Fort Toulouse 25
    Captain Bossu and the Alligator 26
    An Emperor Pays a Visit 27
    Fort Tombecebe 28
    The Coming of the English 29
    Scottish Traders in Alabama History 29
    Alexander McGillivray 31

CHAPTER 4: PIONEER LIFE IN EARLY ALABAMA 35
    The Coming of the Pioneers 36
    Making a Settlement 37
    The Life of a Pioneer 38
    The Pioneer Woman 39
    A Corn Husking 41
    The Circuit Rider 41

CHAPTER 5: CREEK INDIAN WAR 43
    Sam Dale 45
    Indians on the Warpath 47

Sam Dale and the Indians 49
The Massacre at Fort Mims 50
Loyalty 51
Fort Sinquefield 53
Sam Dale and the Canoe Fight 54
The Creek War 56
Sam Dale's Ride 57

CHAPTER 6: STATEHOOD 60
Alabama Becomes Part of the United States 63
Alabama Becomes a State 64
From Territory to Statehood 65
State Seal 65
Alabama's State Song 66
Alabama's Capitols 67
Our Capitol, Montgomery 69
THE "YELLOW-HAMMERS" 69

CHAPTER 7: INDIAN REMOVAL 72
Scottish History in Alabama 74
Chief Doublehead 74
Sequoya 75
The Native Indian Removal 76
Indian Removal Treaties 76

CHAPTER 8: EARLY LIFE ON ALABAMA PLANTATIONS 80
Plantation Life 82
Slave Life on a Plantation 82
Christmas at the Big House 84
Christmas at the Quarters 85
Cotton Picking Time 86
Hog Killing Time 87
Candle Making 88
Soap Making 88
The Slave Quarters 89
The Way the Slaves Dressed 91

CHAPTER 9: YEARS LEADING UP TO THE WAR 92

Events Leading Up to The Civil War 95
CHAPTER 10: WAR BETWEEN THE STATES **100**
   Becoming our Own Country 102
   Music During the War 104
   States that Founded the Confederacy 105
   A Confederate Hospital 106
   The Alabama 107
   Brave Emma Sansom 110
   The Surrender 113
CHAPTER 11: RECONSTRUCTION **114**
   Reconstruction 116
   The Slaves Freed 117
   Freedmen Bureau 118
   Freedman's Bureau & Abandon Lands 119
CHAPTER 12: FREE MEN **121**
   Educating Blacks in Alabama 123
   George Washington Carver: The Strange Story of an Ex-Slave 124
   The Story of Maria Fearing 126
CHAPTER 13: THE SPANISH-AMERICAN WAR **129**
   The Spanish-American War 130
   Fighting Joe Wheeler 130
   Hobson and His Brave Companions 133
CHAPTER 14: WOMEN OF COURAGE **135**
   A Tiny Poet 137
   The Story of Helen Keller 140
CHAPTER 15: WORLD WARS **145**
   The World War - The Army 146
   The World War the Navy 147
   The World War Life in America 149
   The First American Hero of the World War 150
   After The War 151
   A General Who Saved Millions of Lives: William Crawford Gorgas 152
CHAPTER 16: POWER GENERATION IN ALABAMA **157**
   MUSCLE SHOALS 159

The New Deal..........161
Alabama Power Company..........162
CHAPTER 17: CIVIL RIGHTS MOVEMENT..........**163**
The Fight for Freedom..........165
Share Cropping..........165
Jim Crow Law..........166
The Freedman's Right to Vote: Poll Taxes..........167
Literacy Test for Voters..........167
"Grandfather Clauses"..........168
Property Ownership..........168
The Scottsboro Boys..........168
Tuskegee Airmen..........168
Bus Boycotts..........169
School Desegregation..........170
Church Bombing in Birmingham..........170
CHAPTER 18: SPACE & ROCKET PROGRAM IN ALABAMA..........**171**
Wernher von Braun..........172

CHAPTER 1
GEOGRAPHY

Vocabulary:

Fertile	Region	Sapling
Precipitation	Humidity	Temple
Ornaments	Meteorologist	Territory
Civilization	Citizen	Bountiful

Research Suggestions:

1. The Native American culture passed their family history down by storytelling from generation to generation. You are going to learn to note your way through Alabama history on your timeline. You can also note or journal the activities in your daily life. This will help you create your own family stories that you could one day pass down to the next generation. Begin your notebook journaling of daily studies today!

2. Research the population of Alabama and your county. Find out the area of the state and your county measured in acres. Now you can compare the size of anything you study to our state and your county; this will help you understand the size in comparison.

For example:

Populations:
Lauderdale County   State of Alabama
87,422   4,464,356
Acreage:
428,480   32,480,128

> **Example of how to use this comparison formula**
>
> At the battle of Gettysburg 51,100 people died in 3 days. This is the equivalent of well over half the population of Lauderdale County dying at Gettysburg.
>
> You could compare deaths on The Trail of Tears to your county size or even compare it to the amount of land/acreage taken from the Native Americans. You could also compare death totals at the Battle of the Bulge to the population in your county.

3. Make a list of the ways in which Indian boys and girls were trained.

4. What are some of Alabama's natural resources? How do these resources affect our economy?

5. What were some of the Native American tribes that lived in your area of the State of Alabama?

6. List the tribes that originally made their homes in Alabama.

Science & Nature Study:

1. Research the following:

Flax	Sassafras	Pearls
Mullein	Burdock	Gourds
Muscle Shells	Passion Flower	Hickory

2. Research the following wildlife native to Alabama. When did the Yellow Hammer become the state bird?

Yellowhammer	Bear	Marten
Deer		

Project suggestions:

- Research basket weaving. Make a basket using the same/similar methods; materials and techniques American Indians would have used to make their baskets.
- Research the art of pottery and make a bowl.
- Make a sand table showing some of the mounds you might find in Alabama built by the mound builders.
- Make a list of things that might be found in the mounds.

Additional Reading Suggestions:

Lore of the River: The Shoals of Long Ago by Dr. William L. McDonald
ISBN # 978-1-934610-98-5

Map Work:

1. Mark & label the different geographical regions on your map.

Interior Low Plateau	Red Hills	Delta Shores
Cumberland Plateau	Wire Grass	Piney Woods
Appalachian Plateau	Black Belt	Valley & Ridge
Gulf Coastal Plain	Piedmont Plateau	

2. Mark & label the states that surround Alabama on your map.

Mississippi	Tennessee	Florida
Georgia	Gulf of Mexico	

3. Mark the following rivers on your map.

Mobile Bay	Coosa River	Alabama River
Tombigbee River	Tennessee River	Conecuh River
Mississippi River	Tallapoosa River	Black Warrior River
Chattahoochee River		

4. Mark these cities or towns on your map.

Moundville	Danville	Florence

5. Mark the Indian mounds in Moundville and Florence on your map. Locate the Indian mounds in the Southeast part of the state; mark those on your map.

Student Workbook:

Write in your *Alabama Student Timeline Journal Notebook* the many things you have studied about the mounds and the natives of Alabama.

Alabama the Heart of Dixie

Alabama is a beautiful state located in the heart of the Old South. The states bordering Alabama are Mississippi, Tennessee, Georgia, and Florida. The Gulf of Mexico is south of Alabama. The state lines and boundaries for Alabama have not always been as clear as they are today. We will look more closely at the state lines and how they were determined in Chapter Five.

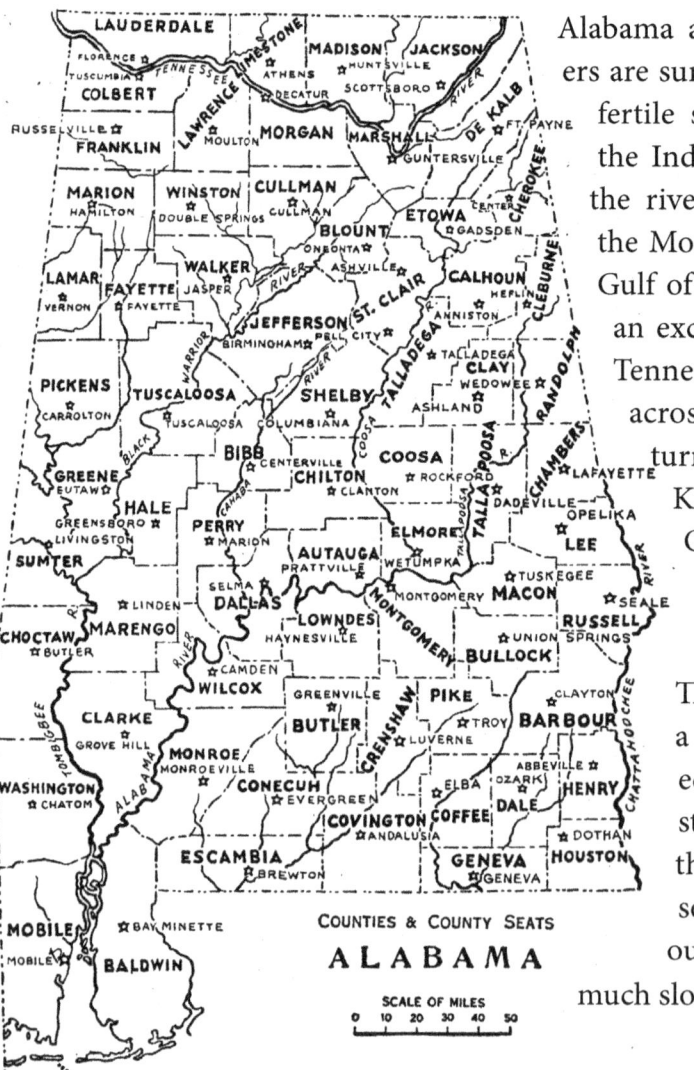

Alabama also has many rivers; these rivers are surrounded by rich fertile soil. The fertile soil around the rivers is where the Indians built their homes. Most of the rivers in Alabama flow south into the Mobile bay, which empties into the Gulf of Mexico. The Tennessee River is an exception to this flow pattern. The Tennessee flows east to west 200 miles across northern Alabama. Then it turns north, up into Tennessee and Kentucky, meeting up with the Ohio, and Mississippi Rivers, which flow south and empty into the Gulf of Mexico.

The rivers of Alabama have played a big part in the settlement and economic development of the state. Without the waterways of these rivers for transportation, the settlement and development of our state would have happened at a much slower rate.

Alabama is a Good Place to Live

Why did people want to settle here? There are many reasons. The climate is pleasant. There is enough rainfall to furnish a steady water supply and to grow crops. The soil is fertile. The creeks and rivers supplied fish to eat and made it easy to go from place to place before roads were built. There are many well-drained and healthy high lands, which will not flood during a wet season, making good homestead locations. There are also many trees that are excellent for building material and plants for food.

Because of the wonderful climate, the wildlife is abundant, providing good food to eat and skins suitable for clothing. We are going to learn as much as possible about the plants and animals of Alabama while studying the wonderful history of our state.

At the southern end of Alabama is Mobile Bay. Most of the rivers in the state empty their waters into the Alabama and Tombigbee Rivers that flow into the Mobile Bay. The Mobile Bay leads out into the Gulf of Mexico and the Gulf of Mexico into the Atlantic Ocean. This connects Alabama to the world by ocean routes.

As you learn more about the geographical divisions in the South, you will understand the significance of the state lines being set up the way they were and for Alabama to have the waterways that currently exist within the state boundary. If things had happened differently, Mobile could have been in Mississippi, which would have economically crippled Alabama. You will learn about this in Chapter Five.

The Mound Builders

Have you ever seen an Indian mound? If you have not, it is very important that you visit one this year. There are still many mounds standing throughout the state. The people who built the mounds are called Mound Builders. Some historians think that the Mound Builders were the ancestors of the tribes known to us as the four tribes of Alabama; others think that they were a different race of people. They lived such a long time ago that nobody knows how they looked. However, by digging into the mounds, we have learned many interesting things about their way of life.

They buried their chiefs with many personal belongings in these mounds. We know that the mounds were built slowly and that many people worked to build them because they did not have machines for digging or trucks for carrying soil.

The Chief's Mound at Moundville, Alabama is 57 feet high covering one and one-half acres of land. It is said that with the tools used it would take 100 men 1,000 years to build the mound. It is believed that the mounds are actually several mounds built up over or around one another over the course of many years and/or generations.

The largest mound in the Tennessee Valley is the one in Florence, Alabama. It is 310 feet from east to west, 230 feet from north to south, and 42 feet high. This is thought to be a temple mound. There are also mounds on the grounds of Oakville Indian Mounds & Education Center in Danville, Alabama. There are many artifacts at the museum.

There are federal laws to protect the mounds now. Yet, prior to the laws to protect the mounds many human remains were found. One was a skeleton of a tall man with that of a little boy lying on his shoulder. Another was a woman with a baby skeleton between her knees. Did these people love their children? How did it happen that these children died at the same time that their parents did? We can imagine many sad stories about these graves.

In addition to skeletons, there have been stone hatchets, stone bowls shaped like birds and turtles found, carved stone pipes, and even heads of people carved in stone and set with copper or gold eyes. Necklaces of shell have also been found, along with beads of jasper and flat copper disks. These beautiful pieces were used to show their love for ornaments. Their skills for making such delicate beauties are definitely magnified in the many pieces available for viewing at mound museums. Beautifully shaped arrowheads show that the Mound Builders were great hunters and warriors.

The Mound Builders were potters also. Pottery has been found in many shapes similar to those of their stone vessels. This pottery was painted white, red, yellow, or black. Why do you think they were buried with these items?

Please take time to visit these museums to learn more about the culture of these people. Although we should always be grateful for the things we can learn from these items, it's just as important for us to respect the law that protects the mounds. When someone digs into a mound it is the same practice as going down to the cemetery and digging someone up. It's a great disrespect to the culture and descendants in addition to breaking a federal law.

Building a Village

Today when making preparations to build a town, there are many important environmental or impact study that must occur before the building process can begin. Once the studies are complete, the leveling of the earth begins, to make it as smooth as possible. The next step in putting up a new building is to dig out a place for a foundation. The early Indians went about building their new town in a very different way. Try to imagine the chief and his warriors standing early in the morning looking toward the east. They would stand as still as the forest, watching from daylight to dawn. As the sun came up, they would wait until the chief felt he had received direction from his sun god for where the new village should be built. Only then would they begin building. The Indians raised a little hill or mound of earth. Around this mound, they made other smaller mounds. This is how the Native Americans would begin their villages.

Sometimes another set of mounds was built just on the edge of the town. These mounds were used as watch places where men would be placed to watch for the coming of enemies. The watchman could see a long way if he stood on a mound. There were many different kinds of mounds used for different reasons.

Many of the mounds have been destroyed by farmers in order to plant corn and cotton. However, some of them stand just as they were when the white settlers came. Farmers have dug up many old things such as bottles, vases, bowls, tomahawks, and knives in and around these mounds. It's impressive that people who had so few tools could create things as nice as the things we have today. It's hard to imagine making such incredibly large tools and bowls without the technology we are accustomed to.

Near the council house in every town was an area where the children played. They played several different types of games. Their favorite sport was a ball game, the game from which lacrosse came. They would often play teams from other towns or villages. On the day before a game, a man would be placed on a high mound or hill outside the town to watch for the visiting players and their friends. When they came into sight, the watchman gave a sign to the people in the town. Yells that we call war whoops filled the air, and the Indians hurried out to welcome the strangers. When the players were all in the field, a big ball was tossed into the air. Each player tried to get the ball. The one who caught the ball tried to make it go between two poles, keeping it in the direction of his town. Then the other players tried it. If a player sent the ball between the poles toward his hometown, he scored. The side making the highest score won the game. A racket like a big spoon was used in the game. It was made of wood with skin or cords stretched over the big part. The players threw and caught the ball with these rackets.

These games were fiercely played, and sometimes competitors were badly hurt or even killed during a game. The game gave the young warriors an opportunity to prove their bravery and ability to endure pain.

Native Americans are still known for their beautiful dances. They used dancing for almost every occasion. Each season of the year had its special worship dance. When Indians went to war, they painted themselves and danced the War Dance. The men always danced; sometimes the women and girls were allowed to join them. These dances gave the Indians wonderful endurance; the dances lasted for hours and sometimes days. The man who danced until everybody else was too tired to go on won great honor.

As time passed, many of the tribes built strong walls around their villages. These walls were made of wood plastered with mud cement and pierced with portholes through which to shoot. At short distances along the walls were watchtowers, which served as lookouts to prevent surprises.

Within the walls was the chief's home; a large wooden house covered with plaster with a long, deep porch in front. The people lived in smaller houses around the chief. There were village kitchens and large village warehouses were filled with skins of bear, deer and other animals. There were also barns filled with dried meat, corn, and vegetables.

The Indians were great hunters. It appears they had no domestic animals before the white settlers arrived, so they depended on game for meat and much of their clothing. They hunted with bows and arrows. Their bows, often eight feet long, were made of hickory and strung with stout strips of hide. Their arrows were made of hickory saplings with points of flint. They were very skillful at stalking game. When hunting deer, the hunter would often stretch a deerskin over wooden hoops, hide inside, and peep through the eyeholes. Then he would creep close enough to a deer to shoot it.

They did not depend completely on game and the wild fruits of the forest for food. We know that they were farmers as well. They dug up the soft soil in the river and creek bottoms with hoes tipped with bone or fish teeth. Then the men made holes with sticks and the women followed, dropping seed into these holes. They grew bountiful crops of corn, beans, squash, pumpkins, and gourds in the rich soil.

In addition to farming, the Native Americans could make baskets, mats, rough cloth, and pottery. When the villagers had more than they needed of these things, they would barter or trade them for something they wanted from another village. The life of the Alabama native was hard, but when the white settlers began to arrive many things changed.

The Native Americans of Alabama were different than the nomadic tribes in the west. By the early 1700's the tribes in the area that would become Alabama lived in villages similar to our rural country towns. They raised gardens for most of their food and hunt for what they did not raise. Most were built very near water, making for plentiful game hunting. Nuts, berries and other vegetation also grow well near the water. Most lived in log cabins much like the white settlers that were first to arrive in the area.

CHAPTER 2
DE SOTO & OTHER EXPLORERS

Vocabulary:

Gauntlet
Sisters of Charity
Haughty

Cirrus
Sinew
Doomed

Colony
Territory

Research Suggestions:

1. Research hominy and how to make it.

2. Make a list of the ways in which Indian boys and girls were trained. What are some of the good things they did as they worked that also strengthened the body?

3. How are "Indian ways" different from our ways?

4. Why was Ortiz so valuable to De Soto?

5. Why do you think De Soto's expedition failed?

6. Bienville tried to make the whites and the red men neighbors. Write five rules which would help people to be good neighbors.

7. Make a list of the difficulties Governor Bienville had as he worked on developing a settlement in early Alabama.

8. What do you think of Alexander McGillivray and the things he did? Do you think he was a loyal man?

People & Places to Research:

Joseph Hare	Juan Ortiz	Fort Toulouse
Tempie Ellis	Iberville	Nancy Glover
Fort Louis	Fort Gaines	De Soto
Governor Bienville	Apalachicola Fort	Tecumseh

Science & Nature Study:

1. How many different kinds of trees grow in Alabama? Can you name some of these trees growing in the state? Do you think the Spaniards knew the names of the trees?

2. Write a report about one of the animals below:

Deer	Eagles	Bear
Fox	Wildcats	Wild Turkey
Wolves		

3. Research some of the plants below:

Persimmon	Mistletoe	Gray Moss
Sweet Bays (also known as Magnolias)		

4. Research these metals:

Gold   Copper

Note: How could you measure their value?

5. Research: Honey Bees and Honey.

Project Suggestions:

1. Candle Making: Melt wax in coffee can, use cotton string. Dip string in wax, wait a minute while it dries, then re-dip; continue until your candle is as large as you would like it to be.

2. Pumpkin: List the many ways you can eat pumpkin. How many things can you make with pumpkin? Make something you enjoy with pumpkin or try a new recipe.

3. Plant a garden with some of the many things the Indians grew.

4. Make persimmon cakes using the recipe given.

5. Draw a picture of the French flag.

6. Draw a picture of what the Alabama Valley of Mobile might have looked like at this time.

> ### Persimmon Cake
>
> 1/2 cup Lard   1/2 tsp Salt   2 Eggs, beaten
> 3 tsp Baking powder   2 cup Sifted flour   1 cup Sugar
> 1 cup Persimmon pulp   1/4 tsp Soda
>
> Cream the shortening and sugar together, add the persimmon pulp and beaten eggs. Sift the dry ingredients and add to the liquid mixture. Beat well, then pour into a greased pan and bake in a moderate oven (325 to 350 degrees) for about an hour.

The Native peoples of Alabama were always glad when persimmons were ripe.

Map Work:

1. Write the names of the Indian tribal territories in their proper places.
Choctaw   Cherokee   Creek
Chickasaw

2. Trace De Soto's journey on the map. Make a list of strange things he might have seen.

3. Put these towns and rivers on the map:
Mobile   Tallassee   Pensacola

Life in the Indian Village

Hernando De Soto was a Spanish explorer and one of the first white men in Alabama. Upon arrival in Alabama, he found many interesting things in the Indian villages. Sometimes the children danced a war dance and painted themselves just as their fathers did. But most of the time they played by hunting in the woods for small game. When Indian boys were still small, they could make traps for rabbits and muskrats. When they grew older, they had bows and arrows with which they hunted small game in the woods. They went on hunting and trapping until they were old enough to have big bows and arrows. Then they were sent out after large game, such as deer and bear. Indian children also fished with lines of deer sinew and hooks made of pieces of bone. The Indian girls helped their mothers plant and harvest corn.

Of course, the Native American children had no schoolbooks, but the boys went to school in the woods. The boys had to learn all the things they would need to know when they grew up. They had to know these things before they became warriors. They would study the habits of birds, rabbits, deer, and many other creature of the forest. They learned how to walk through the woods without making a sound or leaving a track. They learned how to fight to protect their families.

If they left marks on the ground, enemies in wartime would track them and possibly kill them. Indian boys also learned to recognize and distinguish tracks on the ground. They could identify an animal from the tracks. They knew whether a bear, an elk or a panther had passed down the trail. They learned how to make canoes from bark or by digging out trees. They also learned how to paddle them.

Timeline

1507
Mobile bay shows up on a new map published in Europe.

1519
Alonzo de Pineda of Spain, the first recorded voyage into Mobile Bay.

1540-1542
Hernando Desoto, the first explorer in Alabama, arrives.

1559
Tristan de Luna, is the first to try to build a Spanish colony in Alabama.

1607
First permanent English colony in North America was established at Jamestown, VA.

Timeline

1620
Plymouth Colony, established.

1682
La Salle claims all the land draining into the Mississippi River for France, including all of Alabama.

1699
Iberville & Bienville LeMoyne start a French settlement in Mobile.

1702
French settlement builds village on the west bluff bank of Mobile River.

1702
Mobile County, Alabama established, being named after the Maubila Native American tribe.

The boys learned how to endure hunger and fatigue. An Indian might have to walk two or three days through the woods without anything to eat. He was supposed to go on just as if he had eaten and make no complaint.

The boys were taught to bear pain and to show no sign of suffering. An Indian father told his son stories about brave men who could bear pain without crying out. Being able to silently endure pain was necessary to stay safe in the woods. When an Indian boy had learned all these things, the men of the tribe tested him to see if he was a good warrior. If he could bear pain, and prove that he was strong, he was given a name and became a warrior. The Indians trained their young for life, just as many parents train their children in life skills today.

The mothers taught their daughters how to care for a family. They were taught how to raise vegetables and how to cook. They wove beautiful blankets. They made pots and pans out of clay. They made hoes to work the ground. They also tanned and dressed deerskin for their clothes, sewing clothes with thread made of deer sinew and needles of bone. Daughters were also trained to care for the small children and the sick. They lived a busy life and were strong and healthy like the boys. In these ways, young Indians were made ready for life in old Alabama.

Indian Ways

We need many things to make us comfortable and happy. Above all, we must have houses to live in, food to eat, and clothes to wear. The Indians needed these things too, but they did not get them as we do today. Their houses, food, and clothing were quite different from ours.

The habits of different tribes of Indians were not the same. The Alabama tribes—the Creeks, Cherokees, Choctaws, and Chickasaws—in many ways were not alike. At one time, they all lived in the same kind of home. First, they lived in long houses and wigwams made of skin or bark. After a few years, some of the Indian tribes built homes. These homes were log cabins like many of the white settlers lived in. As the chiefs gained wealth, many had homes nicer than some of the wealthy settlers moving into the area.

The Creeks were known for often building two cabins. One was for winter and the other for summer. The summer cabin was just a shelter from rain, open to the air and without a door. The winter cabin was warm and cozy. It was chinked with clay, and there was a door made of skins or boards. A winter house had only one room, where the whole family lived. Father, mother, children, and dogs all slept together in that one room. Beds were made of skins or dried grass laid on the bare ground; the houses had dirt floors. The fire was built in the middle of the room and the smoke went out through a hole in the roof. When they learned to build chimneys, they were then added to the home.

In the midst of the group of cabins that made up an Indian town was an open square, called the town square. Large cabins were built facing this square. Some of the chiefs lived in these cabins.

Near the town square was a house built around a tall pole. This house was large at the bottom, getting smaller and smaller all the way up to a point at the top. The great men of the town met in this house to talk about wars or to make rules for the people to live by. This was the council house. Here the men sat on woven mats while they smoked and talked. Here they settled tribal issues of all kinds. While the men were holding council, the women and children dared not disturb them.

> **Timeline**
>
> **1711**
> The French settlement is relocated to the point along Mobile Bay.
>
> **1714**
> The French build Fort Toulouse in what was to become Elmore County to discourage English expansion.
>
> **1720**
> Perdido River became the boundary between French controlled Louisiana territory which includes Alabama and Spanish controlled Florida.
>
> **1721**
> French bring the first slaves from Africa into Mobile.

Timeline

1736
French build Fort Tombecbee in what became Sumter County to maintain relations with the Choctaws and attack the Chickasaws.

1750
Lachlan McGillivray arrives in the US from Scotland.

1763
British take control of Mobile and rename it Fort Charlotte.

1775-1783
American Revolution establishes the United States of America, governed by the Articles of Confederation.

Juan Ortiz & the Arrival of the Spaniards

Who was Juan Ortiz, who rode beside De Soto? He was not an Indian, although he looked like one. He was a white man of Spanish descent. He had lived so long among the Indians, out in the sun and wind that his skin had became as dark as the natives. He knew their language as well as his own.

When Juan Ortiz was a boy, he became lost in the woods of Florida. His own people could not find him and left him behind when the ships sailed. Some Indians came upon him and made him a prisoner. At that time, he was a white boy, in the clothes of a Spaniard. The Indians did not want him among them. As a result he was given a strange duty to perform. In a lonely spot in the woods was a temple where the bodies of Indians were placed after death. Here they were kept for a time before burial. Ortiz watched day and night to see that wild animals did not steal the bodies. Once he killed a panther that was dragging off a body. He did his work bravely and faithfully, and after a time, he was given a better duty.

The Indians still were not his friends. Once he was made to "run the gauntlet" with some other prisoners. In this sport, the captives ran between lines of men who shot at them with arrows. Ortiz ran so fast that he was the only captive not killed. His swift running made the Indians think better of him.

Later he was given a hut of his own and lived like the Indians. He became a member of the tribe. The chiefs saw that he knew many things and they asked him to come to their councils. Ortiz now painted his body like an Indian and dressed in skin and feathers. He became so much like an Indian that everyone thought he was one.

Then, one day Ortiz heard that white men had landed with boats on the seashore. He was extremely excited; for twelve years he had not seen a white face.

The white men were De Soto and his soldiers. They wanted guides to tell them the way to travel and wanted strong men to carry their loads through the woods. The Spaniards sent out men to capture some Indians for this purpose. One day these Spaniards came across a war party of Indians with Ortiz at the head. Ortiz had been making his way to meet them. The Spaniards carried swords and long spears called lances. They drew these spears and rode toward the Indians. One of them pointed his lance at Ortiz to kill him. To the Spaniard's surprise, the man cried out in Spanish, "I am a Christian! I am a Christian!" The soldier put up his spear, lifted Ortiz upon his horse, and rode back to De Soto's camp. There Ortiz told the strange story of his life. De Soto was kind to him and gave him clothes, a coat of armor, a breastplate, a helmet, and a shield.

Ortiz was just the sort of guide De Soto had wished to have ride with him. He could talk with the Spaniards as well as with the Indians. He knew this strange country and the way to travel. Therefore, Ortiz rode beside De Soto at the head of the line. He was one of the first white men to enter Alabama.

Ortiz had helped the Indians while he lived among them. He knew and respected these people. He always tried to persuade De Soto to treat them fairly. Many times De Soto would not listen to his advice, and much trouble came because De Soto would not listen.

> **Timeline**
>
> **1776**
> Many English settlers in Georgia and the Carolinas opposing the American Revolution flee to Fort Charlotte–Mobile.
>
> **1784**
> Alexander McGillivray makes treaties with the U.S. and Spain at the same time.
>
> **1787**
> South Carolina gives up its claims to area in North Alabama.
>
> **1787**
> United States Constitution is written.

Timeline

1789-1797
George Washington unanimously elected President of the United States.

February 17, 1793
Alexander McGillivray dies on his farm.

1793
Eli Whitney invents the cotton gin.

Coming of the Spaniards

As the Spaniards approached, the watchman of the village announced their arrival to the village. Along the narrow paths came two four-legged creatures wearing covers that glittered in the sun. These were horses covered with armor. The Indians watched horse after horse come into view through the leaves. The Indians did not know what they were, for they had never seen horses before. Then there were priests dressed in the robes of the Catholic Church, bringing with them the crucifix, along with bread and wine for the sacrament, and many other holy relics. There were also soldiers, blacksmiths, carpenters, miners, and other workmen. Following them were packhorses carrying supplies and droves of cows and hogs to furnish milk and meat. It is believed that hogs and horses were first introduced to Alabama by De Soto.

The Indians looked at De Soto and his followers in wonder. Since they had never seen horses before, they thought a horse and his rider were one animal and were much surprised to see the men get off their horses. Remember the horse and rider were wearing armor, which made the two look very much the same. The natives of Alabama knew nothing of guns. It seemed like magic for a gun to make a great noise and an animal at a distance to fall, since they could not see the bullet whiz through the air. The natives had seen very little metal, so the glittering armor of De Soto's men made their shields of animal skins look dull and useless.

Some tribes resisted De Soto. For the most part, however, the Indians were friendly—until they found out De Soto was not a friend. De Soto looked on them as mere savages who were not worth his notice and made many of them slaves to help carry his supplies. He had sailed from Cuba with this intention and had brought chains and handcuffs with him for this purpose.

Although De Soto was proud and cruel, he knew how to be very charming when he thought it was in his best interest. When he reached the Coosa River in Alabama in the spring of 1540, he was all smiles and politeness to the young chief of Coosa, who warmly welcomed him with his beautiful speech: "Mighty Chief! Above all others of the earth! Although I come now to receive you, I received you many days ago in my heart. My person, my lands and my subjects are at your service. I will now march you to your quarters with playing and singing." De Soto then visited the village for several days. He would stay very close to the chief holding him as somewhat of a prisoner to prevent the village from attacking, while his men stole anything they wanted. When he left the village, he would take slaves and stolen goods, leaving the village in devastation. He did this in village after village.

De Soto kept the chief a prisoner in the lodge until he was ready to go on his way again. Then he set the chief free, after making him give the Spaniards some Indians for slaves. These Indians were chained and were made to carry baggage and white men who were too sick to ride. Then the group started on its long march in search of gold toward the West, continuing to take food and slaves in every village they traveled through along the way.

De Soto and the Chief of Tuscaloosa

No messengers welcomed the white men at this place, but they were kindly treated by the Indians. De Soto was surprised to see how the tribe lived. Mobile had around it a great wall of posts and poles. It was so strong that enemies could not enter the town.

The Indians here gave the Spaniards food, but they were not as friendly as the villages before had been. While De Soto was near Mobile, a messenger came asking to speak to him. This is what Ortiz told De Soto:

"Mighty chief, I welcome you to our land. My father, the great chief, bids you come to us at Mobile (or Maubila). He waits for you. We will serve you and your noble warriors well.

Come!" This messenger was the son of Tuscaloosa (or Tuskaloosa), chief of the Mobilians. After he had spoken, he stood with folded arms waiting for the Spaniard to reply. De Soto had Ortiz speak words of thanks to him and he gave the lad some presents, one of which was a scarlet robe. Then the young Indian went away. He sent Moscoso, the captain of his soldiers, and some of his best men to meet Tuscaloosa and try to make friends with him.

Tuscaloosa

Moscoso found Tuscaloosa on a hill about thirty miles to the south of Tallassee. A large mat had been spread on the ground. On the mat were two beautiful cushions, and on the cushions sat the largest Indian the white men had ever seen. Painted warriors stood beside him. Four men held a cover over him to keep off the sun. This cover was shaped like a square umbrella. It was made of deerskins and painted many colors.

Moscoso got off his horse and spoke to Tuscaloosa. The chief did not answer him. Tuscaloosa knew that Moscoso was not the head of the Spaniards; he would not speak to anyone but De Soto. Moscoso showed him the horses and tried to make friends with him. He offered him gifts. However, the chief acted as if he did not hear the Spaniard. Moscoso had to go back without having talked with him. Later, De Soto came up with the rest of his men. Then Tuscaloosa rose and spoke. He invited the Spaniards to go with him into Mobile, which was his town. Again, De Soto was afraid. He thought he must keep this big Indian where he could be seized if he became angry. He commanded that the largest horse in his army be brought for the chief to ride. Since Tuscaloosa wore a red robe and a red cap, a red cover was put on the horse. The Indian chief was so tall that his feet nearly touched the ground. How strange he must have felt on horseback, for he had never been on a horse before!

As the Spaniards rode toward Mobile, they passed through beautiful country. De Soto tried to talk to Tuscaloosa, but the big chief would only grunt now and then. He saw that De Soto meant to keep him a prisoner, and this made him angry. The Mobilian warriors were also angry at De Soto's treatment of their chief, but the Spaniards were afraid to release Tuscaloosa.

A wooden wall that surrounded the village was covered with mud. The mud gave the wall a look much like a stone wall. All along the path, the Indians were coming and going. Many of them waited before the gate of the town. De Soto, Juan Ortiz and Tuscaloosa rode up to the gate. The horses frightened the Indians for a moment, for they had never seen a horse.

Tuscaloosa welcomed the visitors. When he finished speaking, the air was filled with wild whoops and the music of cane flutes. Beautiful maidens led the white men through the gate to the public square. A mat had been spread in the council house. Here De Soto and Tuscaloosa sat under a canopy of furs. The other Spaniards rested in the square. A feast was held, and the Indians danced in honor of the visitors.

However, Tuscaloosa had little to say. This frightened De Soto and he tried to win Tuscaloosa with flattery. For a time the chief listened to him in silence. Then, suddenly, he cried out in a voice that could be heard by all. He demanded that he be allowed to go where he pleased in his own town. Rising, he walked away and hid himself. The Spaniards did not dare stop him.

A warrior led De Soto to the hut made ready for him. De Soto had a feast prepared, to which he invited Tuscaloosa. The messenger returned with a message that sent terror to the hearts of the Spaniards. The chief would not come, and he replied that the sooner the strangers left his town the better.

The white men knew that trouble was at hand. Soon an Indian ran into the square, crying out that the strangers were cruel robbers. A Spaniard killed him as he was speaking. The Indians and Spaniards began running out of the houses. A terrible fight had begun. The Spaniards had to get away from the town, leaving their prisoners and supplies inside. Many white men were killed, as well as a great many Indians. De Soto had only a part of his army with him, as Moscoso (remember Moscoso was De Soto's camp manager) and his men were not with him at Mobile. The Indians closed the gate of the town.

Later Moscoso came with his soldiers; De Soto tried to overthrow and take Mobile. The Spaniards tore the mud from the walls and set fire to the wood beneath. The walls burned and the flames spread to the houses. When morning came, the village of Mobile was a heap of ashes and Tuscaloosa was dead.

De Soto was wounded in the fight. As soon as he was able to travel, he set out toward Mississippi still searching for gold. They did not find gold but they did find the Mississippi

River. De Soto never recovered from his injury from the battle at Mobile. He died after reaching the Mississippi, and his men buried his body near the river. That was the end of De Soto, the first white man ever to set foot in Alabama and Mississippi.

It was over 162 years after De Soto's expedition before there is any other account of white people in Alabama. The battle of Mobile had destroyed the power of the Mobilian Indians.

By 1702, there were four primary tribes in Alabama. It appears the Chickasaws, Choctaws, and Creeks were all Muscogees. The Cherokees were the fourth tribe, with strong roots all the way over into North Carolina. The Costa, Coosa and the Mobilians that were mentioned above were villages of Creek. The Creeks were the most powerful tribe in the Alabama area for many years. They actually controlled over two-thirds of the land that is now Alabama.

The Cherokees lived along the banks of the Tennessee River. The Chickasaws were to the Southwest along the upper Tombigbee River. The Choctaws were south of the Chickasaws. The Creeks were in the East along the Coosa, Tallapoosa, and Alabama rivers all the way to Mobile.

CHAPTER 3
FRENCH & ENGLISH

Vocabulary:

Luxury
Festooned
Timber
Pillion
Forest

Research Suggestions:

1. Learn to use your library's genealogy department. See what you can learn about some of the people or places listed below.

2. There had been four flags flown over Alabama soil up through the time of the Revolutionary War. What four countries did these flags represent? Draw them in your *Alabama Notebook Timeline Journal*.

3. Forts where built along many of the rivers. Why were the forts on the rivers? Could you take a print out of state of Alabama and begin marking the areas that the forts were built?

People & Places to Research:

Fort Tombecbe
Tombigbee River
Fort St. Stephens
Coosa River
Alabama River
Tallapoosa River

Science & Nature Study:

Thunder
Live Oak
Gray Moss
Lightning
Pine
White Oak
Mistletoe

Coming of the French

In 1702, many French people decided to come to Alabama. They came not only to hunt for gold, but also to make settlements. King Louis XIV of France was, at that time, the greatest king in the world. He claimed the country for France and named it Louisiana after himself. He sent out a French nobleman, Iberville and his brother Bienville, to make settlements in Louisiana.

As they were sailing along the coast of the Gulf of Mexico, they found the beautiful bay of Mobile Bay, named after the Mobilian Indians. The climate was warm and there were forests of pine for building ships and a large river emptied into the bay. As they continued to explore, they found that this river was formed by what we know as the Alabama and Tombigbee rivers; this river was named Mobile River.

Iberville decided to send his brother, Bienville, to build a town on Mobile River near the bay. First, he had to build a fort. This fort, Fort Louis de la Mobile, was built of pine logs. Then log houses were built for the men to live in. The Indian tribes around Mobile Bay were weak, and the French were very friendly; so they did not need a wall around the town. Built in the fort on the north side was the first church in Alabama. It was a Roman Catholic Church, and French priests sent out by the king of France held the first services.

Mobile grew very slowly, although the king provided cows, horses, hogs, and fowls to help stock the colony. With hard work, the colonists could grow crops; but the warm climate made them lazy, and there was much sickness. Food was often scarce, so no wonder the men became discouraged. Many of the men had hoped to find gold, and many were wood rangers, or traders in pelts. These gentlemen did not make good settlers. It was decided that, if the settlement was to be successful, the men must have homes. How could they have homes unless they had wives? The king ordered twenty-three young women of good families, under the care of four Sisters of Charity, to be sent to Mobile to marry these men. They came on a ship called the Pelican. Each girl brought a chest with supplies of linen for housekeeping. So they were called "the girls of the chest."

Bienville told the men that these young women were coming, but no one could marry one of the young ladies until he had a house to live in and could take care of a wife. They began to work, and soon all of the girls except one had a husband and a home.

Petticoat Rebellion

The young ladies had a hard time adjusting to the new area. These ladies were just that—ladies. They had been trained to cook and keep house in France. One day the ladies gathered together and went to see Bienville. They were so upset because they didn't know how to cook with the things available in the Mobile area. Bienville had his personal cook work with the young ladies to help them learn to cook with corn meal, seafood, and herbs from the woods. They were much happier once they knew how to cook.

With hard work, the little settlement grew until 1711, when the Mobile settlement was flooded for a month. The people had to take their livestock to higher land, and some had to take refuge with the neighboring Indians; but most of them huddled together inside the fort.

After this, there was only one thing to do, and that was to build a new settlement on higher ground. A place was chosen on the west bank at the mouth of the Mobile River, and a fort was built where the city of Mobile now stands. Here the town began to grow, especially after slaves were brought in to do the heavy work.

Although there was plenty of land around Mobile, the streets were narrow and houses were built close to the sidewalks in French fashion. Most of the houses were one-story frame houses. Some of the houses were plastered with oyster shell filled plaster. Glass for windows was scarce in France. Thus in Mobile the windows were without glass and were closed by solid wooden shutters. In a court at the back of the house, there were vegetable and flower gardens. The men worked taking care of the family and their wives and the church made their life pleasant.

The Building of Fort Toulouse

Life was not always peaceful at Mobile. The English and the French were fighting in Europe; as a result, they were not friendly with one another in America. This made trouble with the Native Americans because both countries worked hard to maintain good relations with them in hopes to keep trade open for economic reasons. The French decided that they must build a fort in the eastern part of the Louisiana territory (remember Alabama was once part of the Louisiana territory) to increase their trade with the Indians and to keep the English traders out.

It is easy to imagine what the French saw as they traveled eastward up the Mobile and Alabama rivers. The woods were full of many kinds of trees: pines, magnolias, sweet bays, and oaks thick with mistletoe and festooned with long, gray moss. All along the streams were wildflowers, flowering vines, and birds of many kinds. Deer and foxes, wolves, wildcats, and bears were wandering through the woods; and Indians were everywhere. When the French reached the headwaters of the Alabama River, where the Coosa and the Tallapoosa meet, they built a fort on the Coosa and called it Fort Toulouse, after a son of King Louis XIV.

Captain Bossu and the Alligator

Captain Bossu, a French captain, was visiting forts in the area that is now known as Alabama. He and his men were in the habit of tying their boats after darkness came and going ashore to sleep. Because there were many mosquitoes on the riverbanks, the hunters made tents in which to sleep. First, they laid a skin on the ground for a bed. Canes were assembled around this and bent to make the tops touch. Then, a sheet was spread over these.

The mosquitoes could not get in as long as the opening was shut tight. One night, Captain Bossu was lying on the bearskin in his tent. His men had caught some fish for breakfast and the fish were in his tent. Captain Bossu was suddenly awakened. It was very dark. He rubbed his eyes and thought he must be dreaming. Something was dragging his tent away, pulling him along with it, along with the bearskin on which he lay! He yelled for help. The soldiers made a light to see what was going on. They called to Captain Bossu to get out of the tent quickly. He jumped out. Then—splash! Into the river went the tent! A huge alligator had smelled the fish and tried to get them. It had taken hold of the bearskin with its teeth, pulling and pulling until it pulled the tent and all into the river. Captain Bossu was glad that the alligator had not pulled him into the water too!

An Emperor Pays a Visit

At Fort Toulouse, everyone seemed to be busy. Just from observing all of the work being done to prepare for the coming guest; it was clear that someone important was to arrive. There were people cleaning, the table had been set for a feast, and the cooks had been busy for several days. Captain Bossu, who was at the fort, took some of his soldiers and went out to meet the guests. When he saw the large party of visitors, he was glad the dining table was long.

The guests were Indians, with their bodies painted in all colors and with feathers standing high on their heads. On one horse, a spotted skin was fastened under a rich saddle that had come from England. On the saddle sat the youngest man in the party. He was only eighteen years old. He wore a scarlet coat with shiny lace down the front and on the sleeves. The young man was an emperor of the Creek. (An emperor is a ruler similar to a king.)

A wise old man rode by the emperor. This man was always with him to advise and help him. Just as Captain Bossu took the emperor's hand, the soldiers fired their guns, making a loud noise. It was the signal for the men back at the fort to fire the cannon. This pleased the Indians.

The guests were delighted with everything that had been prepared for them at Fort Toulouse. They had an interpreter who helped them to talk with the French. The second day of their visit, a party was given at the governor's house. The Indian visitors were greatly pleased when they saw the soldiers lined up to welcome them.

The happiest time came when they sat down to a big table covered with roast turkey, boiled meats, bread, and many other good things to eat. The Indians did not understand the white man's table manners. Even the emperor did not know what to do with his knife and fork.

The emperor's servant, who stood behind his chair to serve him, could not tell him how to use them. The wise old friend of the emperor, anxious to do the best he could, took up a leg of turkey in his hands and broke off a piece of the meat. "The Master of Life made fingers before he made knives and forks," he said. The servant behind the emperor's chair saw the white men spread a yellow mixture on their meat. None of the Indians had tried it, and the servant was curious to know about it. He could speak a little French, so he asked what the mixture was.

Without speaking, the Frenchman handed him a spoonful of the yellow stuff. The Indian swallowed it in one gulp. The next moment he gave a whoop that brought everybody in the fort running to the spot. Yell after yell burst from him. My, how that mustard burned!

The Indian thought he was poisoned and was going to die. The governor finally made the poor fellow stop yelling by giving him a cool drink. The French soldiers must have had to laugh quietly, because they knew the man was not poisoned. Once his mouth quit burning, he knew the Frenchman had not tried to kill him. This visit was one of many of the visits the French and natives of the area had with one another.

Bienville

Fort Tombecebe

To keep the trade along the Tombigbee River and to protect their friends; the Choctaw Indians and Bienville built a fort on the Tombigbee River and called it Fort Tombecebe. The Chickasaw Indians were enemies of the Choctaws and were not pleased with having the fort on the Tombigbee River between them. After having so much trouble with the Chickasaw over the fort,

Bienville decided that he would fight the Chickasaws. A large number of men, from New Orleans, Mobile and other French settlements, joined Bienville's troops at Tombecebe. Bienville had plenty of biscuits and other food prepared for the soldiers. A barrel full of biscuits was ready, and yet there was not enough to feed them.

The war was far from being a picnic. Very few of Bienville's men were trained soldiers. The Choctaws also had little training in war. The Chickasaws had captured a French force from the north that Bienville had expected to join him. The weather was very wet, and Bienville's troops could not bring in cannons. The men grew discouraged. Many of the French were killed, and Bienville returned to Mobile very disappointed over the defeat. He did not give up, however, and some time afterward, he returned and defeated the Chickasaws.

Later Bienville lost his position of governor. He returned to France and lived to be ninety years old. He always felt an interest in Mobile and would ask eagerly for news whenever a ship came from the Louisiana Territory to France.

The Coming of the English

The English won the war with France. When peace was made with France, Louisiana was given to the English. The King of England declared that the eastern part of the Louisiana territory that is now Alabama should no longer be called Louisiana. It was at this time that the area that is now Alabama became part of Georgia. With the southern area around Mobile, he established a separate colony and named it West Florida. Trade between Georgia, South Carolina and West Florida grew to be important.

Scottish Traders in Alabama History

Alabama has a very rich Celtic history. The Scottish first came to Alabama as traders. These traders were better received by the Indians than their competitors, the French traders, because the Scottish traders were assimilated into the tribes. Living among the Native Americans, the Scottish traders married into the tribes. Later on we will study some chiefs that are half Scottish.

Operating a trade business bringing things in and out of the Alabama in the early 1700's was very difficult.

Waterways were, of course, used for transportation if possible, but not all places could be reached by water. Trading by land was difficult because the roads were only rough trails widened by use. Goods had to be carried from place to place by caravans of mule trains. These mules were hardy and accustomed to bearing heavy loads. A pack was fastened on each side of a mule and another pack on his back.

What might we find if we took a look into one of the packs a mule was carrying? Coming from the Indian country, the packs contained many pelts. Since money was scarce, items were valued as being worth *so many buckskins* instead of dollars. Besides pelts, there were beef tallow and bayberry wax for making candles, and sacks of wheat, corn, and dried meat. After the goods were delivered to Mobile, the mules would carry back cloth, trinkets and firearms.

The mules were very intelligent. Whenever Indians were near, they would lift their heads, snort, and seem uneasy. Then they would face the direction from which danger was coming and throw their ears forward. Their ears were as good as a compass to the trader. The mules were such alert animals that their owners relied on them to give a warning of the approach of an enemy. This was important since the tribes, even in Alabama, were often warlike.

There were few bridges. When a stream was too deep to ford they would cross on rafts. These rafts were made of two bundles of willow poles placed several feet apart, with a floor of poles laid across and fastened to the bundles. The packs would be taken off the mules' back and loaded on the rafts. Then the mules plunged into the stream, swam across, and stood patiently waiting on the opposite bank until they were loaded again. The traders would pole or paddle the rafts over the streams, often at the risk of the rafts being tipped or flipped by a snag and their goods damaged or lost.

You must not think that the Indians were the only enemies of the traders. There were other mounted riders on swift horses that would hide and wait for the caravans, then rush out on them, steal their goods and often kill the owners if they resisted. They would then carry off the supplies. There was a famous robber named Joseph Hare who kept his loot in a cave called Turk's Cave. He and his men would attack caravan after caravan until they had a large supply of goods. Then they would carry their loot to Pensacola in the Spanish country and sell it for Spanish silver.

Alexander McGillivray

One day some packhorses were starting toward Charleston, South Carolina. Young Alexander McGillivray, half Creek and half Scottish, was riding beside his father. He was 10 years old at the time, but would someday be the chief of his village. His father felt it was very important for him to have a formal education. He could receive this education in the catholic schools in South Carolina.

Alexander's father was not Indian, but Scotch. He had lived in Scotland until he was thirteen years old, when he ran away and worked his way to America on a ship. When he stepped from the ship in South Carolina, he had only one little piece of money in his pocket. He needed to find work at once.

He stood there, wondering what to do. Just then, dark-skinned men came by, driving horses with heavy packs on their backs. Someone told him that these horses were taking food and clothes to the wilderness homes of Indians. The Indians were glad to have the strong lad with them to help with the horses.

This boy's name was Lachlan McGillivray (Lock-lan Mac-Gill-vray). He went with these Indians to a place in Georgia, where he made his home with the Creek tribe. When he grew up, he married a beautiful Indian girl. She was of the tribe of the Wind, the best tribe of the Creeks. She was from a wealthy Creek family. She loved her husband and children, and made a beautiful home for them near the Coosa River. Their little town was called Little Tallassee. She named her baby boy Alexander and her two girls Sophia and Jeannette.

Lachlan McGillivary made money and in no time he became rich. He wished to do the best thing for his children. When Alexander was older, he took him away to school.

Alexander learned fast. He soon knew so much that his father came to take him away to work in a store in Georgia. Alexander did not like this kind of work. He spent his spare time reading and studying as many books as he could find.

Then his father decided to allow the boy to attend school longer. He carried Alexander to another school in South Carolina. There the lad studied hard, learning several languages.

During these years, Alexander sometimes was able to go back to Tallassee to visit his mother and sisters. After he returned to school, he would shut his eyes and seem to hear the murmur of the Coosa River, which ran near his home. At night, he became homesick. He dreamed of swimming, of shooting arrows, as well as hunting and fishing.

However, he did not go back until he had learned everything his teachers could teach him. The Indians were glad to have him among them. They enjoyed listening to the things he told them. They made him the great chief of the Creeks.

Alexander McGillivray knew how to deal with people; that is, he knew how to persuade them. Alexander had developed bad character and a selfish spirit. He was only thinking of his own needs, not the needs of his people.

You must remember that at this time there were French in Alabama, Spaniards in Florida, and Americans in South Carolina and Georgia.

Sometimes, McGillivray scared the French people and made them do as he wished. Sometimes he teased the Spaniards. He made everyone who had any dealings with him pay him money and do things for him. The Creeks would fight when he told them to fight.

The Creeks wished to continue to have access to their hunting lands, which the white people of America wanted. Settlers in Georgia met the chiefs of the tribe and tried to buy the land, but Alexander McGillivray wished his people to keep the land. This caused many bad feelings between the whites and the Creeks.

Americans in the states north of Alabama also wanted to buy the land. George Washington was President of the United States at that time. He sent men to talk with McGillivray about the sale of the land, but they failed to get his consent for the sale.

At last, President Washington sent Colonel Willett to see what he could do. McGillivray went to meet him with two thousand warriors. Colonel Willett treated the Indians in a kind way, and they listened to what he had to say. Then McGillivray gathered the chiefs together to talk it over.

While Colonel Willett was waiting to hear what the Indian council would do, he spent the time visiting. He went to see what was left of old Fort Toulouse and found most of it in ruins. He went to Little Tallassee, where Alexander McGillivray had lived with his beautiful Indian mother. He also visited Coweta and an interesting place called "a city of refuge." Among the Indians, if anyone did wrong, he could go to this "city of refuge." As long as he stayed there, no one could punish him.

Colonel Willett came back to the town where the chiefs and McGillivray waited for him. He brought them a pleasant surprise. It was an invitation from President Washington!

Alexander McGillivray and all his chiefs were invited to go to New York. There the Great White Father (as the natives would call him), George Washington, desired to speak to them. McGillivray and the chiefs talked it over. Hollowing King, a big Indian, gave the answer to the invitation. This is what he said: "We are glad to see you. You have come a great way. As soon as we fixed our eyes upon you, we were made glad. We have not the knowledge of the white people. We were invited to the treaty at Rock Landing. We went. Nothing was done. We were disappointed and came back with sorrow. The road to your great council house is long and the weather is hot; but our beloved chief shall go with you and such others as we shall appoint. We will agree to all things that our beloved chief shall do. We shall count the days he is away, and shall be glad when he comes back. We shall be glad to see a treaty that will be as strong as the hills and as lasting as the rivers. May you be preserved from every evil!"

The journey from Alabama to New York was a long one. Alexander McGillivray, the chiefs and Colonel Willett, rode all the way on horses. President Washington met them in New York. The Indians were taken to see all the sights and were given presents.

There was much talk and the U.S. government paid the Creeks money for their land. Alexander McGillivray had become a very bad man over the years he kept most of the money for himself. But he persuaded the Indians to give up the land. But that is not all that he did, he also sold the same land to the Spanish that were in Florida and the French that occupied the area west of them.

To make the situation worse, he did not share this money with his Creek people. He kept the most of it for himself. The three countries became very upset with him. His people sent him away from the fellowship of the village and the friends he had always known. He had disgraced himself and his people. He lived the last years of his life in disgrace, a very lonely man. He was no longer the powerful chief he had been for many years. His father would have been very disappointed.

CHAPTER 4
PIONEER LIFE IN EARLY ALABAMA

Vocabulary:

Luxury	Circuit	Catholic
Festooned	Protestant	Pillion

Research Suggestions:

1. Learn to use your library's genealogy department. See what you can learn about some of the people listed below.

People & Places to Research:

Fort Tombecbe	Fort St. Stephens	Lorenzo Dow
William Bartram		

Science & Nature Study:

Thunder	Live Oak	Tornado
Lightning	White Oak	

Local & Family History:

Go to your local library's genealogy room and look up information about your city/county and family. Call your grandparents and older family members to learn what you can about the family.

1. Research the history of the U.S. Post Office. When did the local Post Office in your hometown first begin operation? Add this information to your *Alabama Timeline Journal Notebook*.

The Coming of the Pioneers

You have read about the traders that came to Alabama, but not all the people who came to Alabama in those early days were traders. Many wished to make homes. These were settlers, often called pioneers. Since travel was dangerous in the Indian country, it was custom for a number of people to plan to make the journey together for protection.

If there were roads, they were rough and full of tree stumps. Some of the pioneers walked, some rode on horseback with their wives and children on pillions behind them. Many times a man or his family trudged along beside a yoke of oxen hitched to a pole that had been struck through a great hogshead that carried their goods. Some had covered wagons drawn by oxen or horses. The boys and men drove the cattle and hogs while the dogs followed. There were still no bridges across the streams. If there was not a place to ford or if the waters were too high, the animals swam, pulling the wagon behind them. Most of the time people crossed the water in their wagons or on horseback; sometimes they used logs, rafts or canoes.

Pioneers on the Road

The journey was long, and only a few miles could be covered each day. When the party camped at night, they built a fire to cook supper. Making a fire was not a simple task. Matches had not been invented, and fires were started either by rubbing sticks together or by striking flint with iron. You can understand how hard it was to make a fire when the wood was wet.

Supper was a very simple meal of cornbread made of cornmeal, salt, and water. It was called ashcake if cooked in hot ashes, or Johnnycake if baked on a hot stone in front of the fire. Sweet potatoes were baked in the ashes and meat was cooked on sticks over the fire.

The livestock would be rounded up and fed. Of course, some of the men had to keep watch in shifts during the night. While the campers ate and rested, they told stories about the homes they had left or about what they had heard they could expect in the Alabama wilderness. Someone in the party was sure to have a banjo, or at least a mouth harp or Jew's harp. So they would play, sing, and perhaps dance a jig.

Where would the pioneer families sleep? What sort of shelter could be found in these wild woods? Those who had covered wagons were well sheltered, but those who did not tried to stop at night where they would be sheltered by overhanging rocks or perhaps a cave. When the weather was favorable, a bed of leaves and blanket might be good enough. However, when it rained, a tent made of poles covered with blankets, quilts, or skins would be used. At daybreak everybody was out of bed. Breakfast was very much the same as supper. In fact, there was very little variety in their food, except that venison, opossum, or wild turkey might take the place of bacon or other cured meat from day to day.

If any member of the party died, he had to be buried by the side of the road with only a few stones to mark his lonely grave. Yet, in spite of hardship, struggle, and danger, the pioneers came and continued to come to this new country.

Making a Settlement

These first settlers did not need to buy land. Each man cut the trees surrounding his claim and laid down the first four logs of a cabin. Life was hard; but the pioneers were committed, and each helped the other. The houses consisted of one large room with an earthen floor. Wooden pegs were used for nails, and the doors were hung on wooden hinges fastened with wooden latches. Since there was no glass, the windows were protected by heavy wooden shutters. Overhead there might be a loft, which could be reached by wooden pegs in the wall, and entered by a trap door.

Large fireplaces gave warmth and cheer to the home, and took the place of a stove for cooking. Pots, pans, and skillets were hung beside the chimney and across the front fireplace on long rods and pothooks. Plates were made of wood and drinking cups of gourds, unless the pioneer was lucky enough to have brought a little crockery or pewter from his old home. As gardens were harvested, the ceiling was filled with strings of red peppers, onions, tobacco, and herbs. Their seats were benches made of split logs on pegs. In a corner of the room, two walls of the cabin made two sides of the bedstead. The other two sides of the bed were logs stuck from the wall and resting on a forked tree trunk standing on the earthen floor. Either planks or ropes were used as bed slats. A featherbed was a great luxury, when brought all the way from the east, or a shuck sack or mattress completed the bed. Of course, the boys in the attic were glad to get hay or leaves for their bed.

If the family was large or in need of a room for visitors, all that was necessary was to swing a quilt or blanket from the rafters in order to have two rooms.

The Grist Mill

The Life of a Pioneer

The pioneer led a hard, rough life. He had very few tools. A spade, a hoe, or even a pointed stick might be all he had to cultivate the soil. He was fortunate indeed if he owned a plow and mule or an ox. They had no mill in which to grind corn, so they hollowed out a bowl in a heavy piece of wood, and cut pestle from a hickory stick. Then set up a strong forked post, and rested the handle of the pestle in the fork. With this crude machine, he would pound his corn into course meal or grits.

Later, when gristmills were built, farmers carried their sacks of corn to be ground at the mill, paying the miller with part of the corn. They loved to go to the mill because there they would meet up with other farmers. They would catch up on the news and swap supplies such as yarn, eggs, and other goods. Often a store would be built near the mill, and a little village would develop. This store, or trading post, would probably be made of pine logs with only the earth for a floor. For his stock, the storekeeper would have a small amount of course brown sugar at fifty cents a pound, a small amount of green coffee at one dollar a pound, and a few bolts of cloth. These items were hauled to the village in an oxen cart. If the buyer had no money, he could pay with loads of wood or with farm produce.

The Pioneer Woman

A Pioneer Spinning

The pioneer woman worked as hard as the pioneer man. All of her cooking had to be done over an open fire and her washing had to be done at the spring or she had to draw her water from a well. She had to prepare the cotton or wool, dye it, and spin it into thread. She would then weave on a clumsy, homemade loom. Pioneer women would help with the planting of the garden, as well as gathering the vegetables, then prepare them for winter storage. Pioneer women also fed and cared for the chickens and other livestock. The women were as capable of butchering the livestock as they were of cooking it. One of the older daughters would take care of milking the cow, churning the butter, and keeping the dairy products in the nearby spring. The women took care of the sewing by hand, as the sewing machine had not yet been invented. She had to care for the children while they were small. From sun up to sundown, these women were busy!

In addition to all of the other work, a pioneer woman had to be on the lookout for Indians. She had to be able to shoot if needed. If the men of the family were away and unfriendly Indians were to come along; the women of the house would shoot to protect her home.

Children soon learned what to do at such times, and even a young child knew not to cry. Even if they were dropped and hurt, they did not make a sound, for it could endanger their life.

It seems strange that while living like this, the pioneer woman should care for beauty, but she did. She would likely have brought a few flower seeds from her old home, for hollyhocks, sunflowers, and princess feathers often made a bright setting for the tiny cabin. Gourd vines often made graceful frames for doors and porches.

She delighted in weaving and in patching quilts, both for use and for beauty. She made her own patterns and named them from things around her that she loved. The following are some favorite pioneer patterns: The Log Cabin, The Dove in the Window, The Rising Sun, The Star, The Sunflower, The Wild Rose, The Rose of Sharon, and The Circuit Rider.

Every quilt maker in the circuit the preacher preached on made a square for the Circuit Rider Quilt. In the center was the Holy Bible square. This was patched to look like an open book, and the words Holy Bible were written across it in outline stitch.

After the quilts were pieced, the women would meet at one of the cabins and have a quilting. A quilting was a great treat; pioneer women lived far apart, worked hard, and visited little.

The pioneer woman not only made her own patterns but often

Interior of Pioneer Home

dyed her own cloth. If a peddler happened to come by, he was warmly welcomed. His calicos were bright and he brought a fresh supply of thimbles, needles, scissors, and thread. Best of all, he told the news of the great outside world that seemed so far away. It is sad to say but the pioneers had no newspapers, no magazines, and few, if any, books other than the Bible. Even if they had books, there were very few who knew how to read. Therefore, the stranger was given the best the pioneer family could afford and begged to come again.

A Corn Husking

Even with all of their hard work, the pioneers still made time for fun. When the corn was harvested, they would meet for a corn husking. There was a great hunt for a red ear of corn. They believed that the young man or woman who found an ear of red corn would be the next to get married. After a corn husking, there would be someone to play on the fiddle, or the Jew's harp and everybody would dance, sing, and clap to the music.

For refreshments they would enjoy watermelons. If it was the right time of year, opossum and sweet potatoes, wild turkey, deer, bear, hominy and sausage, sorghum pulled candy, and persimmon beer or cider would be among the tasty fare. They had such a good time that they would not stop talking about it until the next corn husking!

The Circuit Rider

Although the early settlers led a rough, dangerous life, there were many among them who were good Christians and wanted to hear preaching. There were others who were wild and lawless and badly in need of hearing the preaching of God's Word. The Catholic priests in the southern part of Alabama did so much good work, both with the white people and with Indians, that there are still a large number of Catholics in and near Mobile, but the settlers had no ministers until the coming of the circuit riders.

Lorenzo Dow was one of the first Protestant preachers in Alabama. He called himself a Methodist; he preached as he felt God had led him to preach. He came from Connecticut, a thousand miles away, on horseback, with his wife Peggy on a pillon behind him. For most of the time, they lived outdoors, sleeping on the open ground.

The Camp Meeting

In many parts of the country, there were no churches. Thus, Lorenzo Dow preached outdoors. He would send word to all of the people within traveling distance to come to meeting. They came in homespun clothes and barefooted, but that did not matter. He would talk very plainly to them about lying, stealing, cheating, and killing. As he preached, he would paint a colorful picture of hellfire so frightfully real, that even the most lawless began to shake. Then he would tell them about the promise of forgiveness for sins if they would repent and follow Jesus.

There was much excitement, and many praises to the Lord! Those who had asked forgiveness were very thankful to the Lord and the circuit preacher that had shared the good news of Jesus. The new Christian and their friends would shout, "Hallelujah! Bless the Lord!" Some of these people who "came forward" during a meeting later forgot their promise to be godly and were said to backslide. Many of them, however, continued to live dedicated Christian lives.

These meetings out in the open not only encouraged the early settlers because of the opportunity to fellowship with other Christians, but they were a great pleasure to them also. At camp meetings, those who lived in one settlement would meet those who lived in another. They enjoyed talking about everyday things just as you and I do. Families would share lunches and the young people would meet others their age. Often a young couple would meet one year at a camp meeting and then marry the next year at the same camp meeting.

CHAPTER 5
CREEK INDIAN WAR

Vocabulary:

Disaster	Faithful	Earnest
Youngest	Brave	English

Research Suggestions:

1. Research the Creek Removal Treaty signed at the end of the battle of Horseshoe Bend. Research the other Creek Removal Treaties that were signed after Horseshoe Bend. How were these treaties different?

2. Research the history of the Creek Nation. Who are some of the interesting Creek people? What did they do to make a difference for their people?

3. Research the Creek War. What happened at Horseshoe Bend? How did this event influence Alabama? How does it affect us today? How much land was surrendered at the end of this war?

4. Who was the U.S. president during the Creek War? Add him to your *Alabama Timeline Journal Notebook*.

5. What is the average distance a horse can travel in a day?

6. What do you think about the family who stood up for their slave and would not let him be whipped? This family could have been murdered by the Indians once they did not have the protection of the fort. What kind of things do you think they were thinking about when they left the fort?

People & Places to Research:

John Donelson	Red Sticks	William McIntosh
John Coffee	Andrew Jackson	Fort Hampton
Sam Dale	General James Wilkinson	Pushmataha
Massacre of Fort Mim	Battle of Holy Ground	McGirth & Sanota
Battle of Horseshoe Bend	Lorenzo Dow	William Weatherford (Red Eagle)

Science & Nature Study:

Research the Following:

Earthquake of 1811	Chestnut Oak	Sleet
Post Oak		

Project Suggestions:

Research one of the above forts and then build a replica.

Map Work:

1. If you were Sam Dale, how long would it have taken you to travel from your home to Georgia on a horse?

2. How many hours would it take your family to travel to Georgia in your car?

3. Mark & label Horseshoe Bend on the map.

4. Mark & label Wetumpka.

Local & Family History:

Go to your local library's genealogy room and look up information about your city/county and family. Call your grandparents and older family members to learn what you can about the family.

1. Research the name of the first store in your town. Find out what was sold in the store. Add this information to your *Alabama Timeline Journal Notebook*.

Sam Dale

Sam Dale was a real American boy. His father was a pioneer settler. There were seven other children in the family. Sam was the oldest. When he was a small boy, he began to help take care of his brothers and sisters.

Sam Dale found himself at the age of seventeen trying to work out a situation of great responsibility. He had to find a way to take care of his seven younger siblings. His father and mother had just died. His mother passed away and within a short while his father also died. Neighbors helped him bury his parents. The evening after his father's funeral, after everyone else went home, Sam went back out to the graves of his parents. He grieved, and asked the Lord for wisdom and strength to take care of the family.

When he returned home from their graves, he felt more confident about the duties of caring for the family. The next morning he began organizing the children to manage the family farm. He met with all of his siblings. He asked each one of them what they felt they could do to make the home and farm run smoothly. He then delegated duties to each of his siblings. They all had to work hard for the family to survive. The morning after his father was buried; Sam's gift of leadership skills began to be refined and truly tested. His first success as a leader was in his own family. But this was just the beginning of Sam Dale's work as a leader.

When Sam's father died, he owed money on his house and land. Sam wanted to pay back his father's debt. He went to some neighbors to discuss how he might pay his father's debt. They knew he was an honest young man. They all knew how important his success was; he not only had himself to care for, but all of the young children. They told him they would help him learn how to farm. Sam worked from early in the morning until late in

> **Timeline**
>
> **1797-1801**
> John Adams is President of the United States.
>
> **1798**
> Congress creates the Mississippi Territory. Alabama was included in this territory.
>
> **1799**
> Daniel Pratt is born in New Hampshire.
>
> **1799-1801**
> Winthrop Sargent is Governor of the Mississippi Territory.
>
> **1799**
> The U.S. builds Fort Stoddert in Mobile County to protect settlers from the Natives and Spanish.

Timeline

1799
Andrew Ellicott surveys the 31st parallel.

June 4, 1800
Washington County, Alabama is established, being named in honor of George Washington.

1801-1809
Thomas Jefferson is President of the United States.

1801- 1805
William Claiborne is Governor of the Mississippi Territory.

1803
Louisiana Purchase from France increases U.S. Territory.

the evenings and made fine crops. He proved himself as an honest man and everyone was happy to deal with such a fine man.

He paid the money his father owed and then bought a "wagon train." This was different from a packhorse train. Sam Dale's train was a big wagon with a cover over it.

He used it to move people into Alabama. You see, many people were coming into Alabama to find land to settle. As a result, his train was kept busy relocating settlers to their new homes. Traders told people who intended to move to Alabama about Sam. The neighbors were proud of Sam and they were glad to help him by watching out for the younger children while he was away.

Sam's father had left him a flintlock rifle. He carried this rifle beside him while he sat in the front of his wagon and drove travelers through the Indian country. This made them feel safe, but Sam had very little trouble because the Indians liked him and did not try to harm his passengers.

During the winter, Sam drove his wagon and carried many travelers. In the spring and summer, he stopped long enough to do his planting. He made money and after a while, he started a trading post. He traded goods for meat, skins, and other articles the Indians brought to sell. Then he sold these things to the settlers.

Sam Dale was a hard worker. He grew large crops. He always seemed to have more corn than anyone else. Once, he let the United States have a thousand bushels for the soldiers, and he was never paid for it. He raised a great deal of food to give to poor people. He shared his harvest with many Indian villages and took loads of corn to white people who needed help as well. Sam always remembered how much help he received when his parents passed away.

Sam had a wonderful relationship with the Indians, but if he heard that Indians were going to harm settlers, he always helped the settlers. Once, Sam heard that the Indians were going to attack a fort where many women and children had gathered for protection. He knew that most of the men were away and that the Indians would kill the people in the fort. Sam gathered some men to help and hurried to the fort to protect the women and children.

He then received a letter from a general who wrote him to go on to another place with his soldiers. But Sam did not go. He wrote to the general, "There are many women and children here whom I have sworn to defend." He did defend them. Soon the general sent other soldiers to help him.

Indians on the Warpath

Year after year, as more white settlers came into Alabama, many of the Native Americans of the area grew restless and feared they would lose their land. In 1811, a council of Creeks met at Tookabatcha on the Tallapoosa River. Many Cherokee, Chickasaw, and Choctaw chiefs also came to the council meeting. They had heard that Tecumseh, the great Shawnee chief, whose mother was a Creek, would be there to talk his war-talk.

The day the council met, Tecumseh, along with twenty-four warriors, marched into the square where Big Warrior, the Creek chief, and his

Timeline

1803
Federal Road is built between Milledgeville, Georgia and Fort Stoddert, North of Mobile.

1804
John Hunt settles in what becomes Huntsville, Alabama near the big spring.

1805-1809
Robert Williams is governor of the Mississippi Territory.

1806
The Cherokee and Chickasaw give up most of their lands north of the Tennessee River.

War Council

> ## Timeline
>
> **1808**
> Madison becomes the first county in North Alabama named in honor of the 4th American President James Madison.
>
> **February 12, 1809**
> Abraham Lincoln is born.
>
> **1809- 1817**
> James Madison is elected President of the United States.
>
> **1809-1817**
> David Holmes is governor of the Mississippi Territory.
>
> **December 21, 1809**
> Baldwin County, Alabama is established being named in honor of Abraham Baldwin, U.S. Senator from Georgia.

braves were sitting. Tecumseh was handsome, six feet tall and well built; he carried himself proudly. Big Warrior handed a pipe to Tecumseh, who smoked it silently and passed it on to his warriors. Each day, they went through their usual ceremonies, but the two tribes did not say a word to each other. After many days, Tecumseh made his great speech. At first, his voice was sorrowful; then his words were like thunder, and his eyes flashed with hatred. "The Creeks were once a mighty people," he said. "Now your blood is white, your tomahawks have no edge. O, Creek, brethren of my mother, once more strike for your country! Send the white men back to where they came. Burn their homes, destroy their stock, and kill their wives and children. The red man owns this country. War now! War forever! My prophets will stand between you and the bullets of your enemies. When the white men approach you, the yawning earth will swallow them. Soon you will see my arm of fire across the sky; and, at the stamp of my foot at Tippecanoe, the very earth shall shake."

Pushmataha, chief of the Choctaws, made this answer to Tecumseh: "Halt, Tecumseh! Listen to me. You came here as you have often gone elsewhere to stir up trouble between a peaceful people and their neighbors. The Choctaws and Chickasaws are friendly to the white Americans. We have helped them, and they have helped us. Where is a Choctaw or Chickasaw who has ever gone to St. Stephens (St. Stephens was the capitol of the territory) with a worthy cause and been sent away empty handed? We do not take the warpath without a just cause and an honest purpose. You have elected to fight with the English. We are the friends of the Americans. Farewell, Tecumseh! You will see Pushmataha no more until we meet on the warpath."

It happened that some days after Tecumseh had left Alabama, there was an earthquake and a meteor shower. Of course, many of the Native Americans believed that Tecumseh had favor with God. When the earth trembled, the Indians were frightened and believed they should obey him saying, "It is Tecumseh stamping his foot."

The Indians now grew eager to fight. They drank the black liquor, danced the war dance in paint and feathers, and formed a party called Red Sticks for the purpose of getting rid of the settlers.

Sam Dale and the Indians

We must remember many of the Indians were friends to the settlers. Only the Creeks that had chosen to follow Tecumseh were making war. Many of the Creek Indians did not agree with the war. Sam Dale and some other men who were trying to protect the settlers heard of this meeting that Tecumseh had called. They knew he was making plans for trouble. So Sam and his men went to this meeting of the chiefs. Every day they went to the public square, waiting until Tecumseh made his speech.

> **Timeline**
>
> **October 27, 1810**
> West Florida, from the Pearl River to the Mississippi River, is annexed by the U.S.
>
> **May 11, 1811**
> Gazette Newspapers established Mobile, Alabama
>
> **June 14, 1811**
> Harriet Beecher Stowe is born in Litchfield, Connecticut.
>
> **1811**
> Washington Academy established at St. Stephens.
>
> **1811**
> Huntsville, Alabama incorporated.

For twenty-four days they waited. For twenty-four mornings they watched Tecumseh and his warriors come to the meeting. Tecumseh would take a seat, and his Indian followers would wail and wail. This would go on for hours. Then Tecumseh would rise and say, "My children, the sun is now far advanced in the heavens. Wait until another sun for my talk."

The other white men grew tired and went away. Sam Dale stayed and asked an Indian friend to help him keep watch. He and his friend hid themselves nearby, watching and listening. The twenty-fifth day came and Tecumseh thought the white men had all gone away. Then he spoke to the Indians.

Timeline

1811
Tecumseh comes to Alabama encouraging war.

1812
The War of 1812.

1812
Greene Academy is established in Huntsville.

December 10, 1812
Clarke County, Alabama named in honor of Gen. John Clarke of Georgia.

April 15, 1813
U.S. annexes West Florida, from the Pearl River to the Perdido River, from Spain, obtaining Mobile.

July 27, 1813
Battle of Burnt Corn Creek.

What Tecumseh said to the chiefs encouraged them to fight the settlers. They pulled out their knives and waved their tomahawks in the air. Tecumseh talked of war. He told the Indians to fight the Americans who were coming into their country and drive them out.

Sam Dale left the meeting and rode from place to place to spread the news. This helped prepare the settlers for the coming Creek attack. When the Indians began to fight—the Americans were ready! The Indians did not surprise and kill them as they had expected to do.

It took the Americans a long time to defeat the Indians and make them live in peace. There were so many Indians and so few Americans! The Spaniards helped the Indians, and the British watched for a chance to cause trouble for the settlers of Alabama. It seemed as if everyone was against them!

The Massacre at Fort Mims

The settlers became very uneasy because of the Indian uprising, so they fled to nearby forts. Five hundred fifty-five of them gathered in southern Alabama at Fort Mims, near the Alabama River. After waiting and watching for the Indians day after day; the settlers began to doubt the report that the Indians were on the warpath. Colonel Beasley, commander of the fort, became careless and let the heavy entrance gate stay open until a deep pile of sand had drifted up against the gate doors.

William Weatherford, a brave half-Scottish, referred to in his Creek name as Red Eagle, was the leader of the Red Sticks. He was waiting for a chance to seize Fort Mims. He had captured some slaves from Fort Mims, but one of them escaped, ran to Fort Mims, and told Colonel Beasley that Red Eagle was near. After waiting a few days without seeing any Indians, Colonel Beasley said that the black man was a liar. After this, two slaves that were taking care of the cattle in the woods rushed into the fort and said they had seen twenty Indians in the woods. Colonel Beasley sent some soldiers to look for these Indians, but the soldiers returned and reported that they had seen no Indians.

Colonel Beasley decided that the blacks must be whipped for trying to scare everyone by telling untrue stories. One slave was whipped, but the master of the other one said that his slave should not be whipped. This angered Colonel Beasley! He made this man, his family, and slaves leave the fort. When the slave who had been whipped was sent out again to take care of the cattle, he saw more Indians; but due to fear of being punished again, he didn't tell anyone at Fort Mims. He fled to Fort Pierce.

One day at twelve o'clock, when the unsuspecting people at Forts Mims were eating dinner and feeling perfectly safe, wild war whoops were heard! "The Indians—the Indians!" cried the people in the fort. They rushed to the gate to close and bar it, but there was such a pile of sand against it that the Indians were upon them before they could close the heavy gate! Both settlers and Indians fought fiercely, but the Indians won. They killed and scalped without mercy. Only a few whites escaped.

> **Timeline**
>
> **August 30, 1813**
> Massacre at Fort Mims starts the Creek War.
>
> **Nov. 3, 1813**
> The Battle of Tallushatchee.
>
> **Nov. 9, 1813**
> The Battle of Talladega.
>
> **Nov. 12, 1813**
> Sam Dale fights "The Canoe Fight."
>
> **Nov. 18, 1813**
> The Hillabee Massacre.
>
> **Nov. 29, 1813**
> The Battle of Autosee.
>
> **December 1813**
> "The Battle of Holy Ground" or "Econochaca."

Loyalty

Some years before the massacre at Fort Mims, a little orphan Indian boy named Sanota came to Zachariah McGirth's Plantation asking for food. Mrs. McGirth was half Indian

> **Timeline**
>
> **January 22, 1814**
> The Battle of Emuckfau Creek.
>
> **January 24, 1814**
> The Battle of Enitachopco.
>
> **January 27, 1814**
> The Battle of Calabee Creek.
>
> **March 27, 1814**
> The Battle of Horseshoe Bend.
>
> **August 1814**
> Treaty signed at Ft. Jackson between Red Eagle on behalf of the Creek nation and Andrew Jackson on behalf of US government. 23 million acres of Creek land was surrendered to the U.S. Government with the signing of this treaty, opening half of Alabama to white settlement.

herself and was a very kind-hearted woman. She took little Sanota into her home and cared for him just as she did her own seven children. He grew to love her very much. After Sanota was grown, he wanted to live with the Indians and left his kind foster mother.

When Tecumseh talked war talk to the Indians, Sanota listened to him and joined the Red Sticks. During the attack of Fort Mims, Sanota was killing and scalping like the rest of the Indians. He saw before him his foster mother, Mrs. McGirth. As quick as a flash, he ordered her and her children to go into a corner of the fort. Then he stood in front of them to keep the other Indians from killing them by claiming that they were his captives. He told the other warriors he intended to make slaves of them. When the battle was over, Sanota led Mrs. McGirth and her family to a place of safety. He would bring them food and make sure they were okay. Then he would return to make war with the Red Sticks. Before he left for the battle of Horseshoe Bend, he made sure Mrs. McGirth knew the route to travel to make it to Mobile. He told her if he did not return they would not be safe here any longer and they must make their way to Mobile.

Mr. McGirth had been away from Fort Mims when the battle took place; but, as soon as he heard of it, he hurried to the fort. He searched through the bodies at the fort, but he could not recognize any of them as his wife and children. Still, he believed them to be among the dead.

Mr. McGirth moved to his Mobile home. One day when he was working in his office, he was told a poor Indian woman with dirty children was asking to see him. Imagine his joy when he found that this poor woman was actually his wife and that the ragged children were his own!

Fort Sinquefield

The Red Sticks on the warpath decided to send Francis the prophet, a brother of Chief Tecumseh, to attack Fort Sinquefield in Clarks County. On their march, they killed a number of settlers living near the fort and then disappeared.

As soon as the Indians seemed to have moved on, the men at Fort Sinquefield took an oxcart, gathered up bodies of the massacred settlers, brought them to the fort, and began to bury them just outside the walls of the fort.

The women were washing their clothing near the spring, and the children were playing outside the stockade. Charles Phillips, an old man, and Isham Kimbell, a young man, were sitting in front of the gateway talking.

"Look, Isham," said Phillips, "at that fine gang of turkeys on the hill over yonder."

But Isham Kimbell had young eyes.

"Turkey? That is not turkey—it's Indians!" he cried in alarm. The men left their work, caught up the children in their arms, and rushed into the fort. The women were terrified and began to run toward the gate. The Indians, seeing that the women had discovered them, straightened up from the stooping position in which they had been moving along and made a dash for the fort. They had dressed their heads with turkey feathers, bound cow tails on their arms from shoulder to wrist, and were waving the bushy tail ends in the air.

Timeline

September 15, 1814
British attack on Fort Bowyer in Mobile is unsuccessful. Plans to capture Mobile are abandoned as they move on to New Orleans.

1815
First white settlers in Tuscumbia, Alabama

1815
Choctaw Nation gives up all land east of the Tombigbee River.

February 11, 1815
British forces take over Fort Bowyer of Mobile on their return from New Orleans, but abandon it once they learn the war is over.

June 29, 1815
Monroe County, Alabama established, being named in honor of our 5th President, James Monroe.

How were the women saved? Suddenly, Isaac Hayden, one of the settlers, jumped on a horse and began to howl to the dogs around the fort. Approximately sixty dogs rushed out—baying, barking and yelping as Hayden galloped toward the Indians, cracking his whip!

The Indians were surprised by the dogs and had to struggle to protect themselves from the howling pack. The women rushed for the gate, and all but one were saved. The gate had hardly been closed before the attack began. The women molded bullets and loaded guns, while the men fired on the Indians. The fight lasted two hours. One of the Prophets was killed. Then the Indians lost hope, gathered up their wounded and dead, took every horse they could find, and disappeared into the forest.

Fort Sinquefield was saved, but the settlers decided to move to Fort Madison because it was better protected. Of course, they had never heard of an electric light in those days, but Fort Madison was lit in a very clever way. A tall pole forty feet high was set in the ground. Around it was built a platform that could slide up and down the pole. This platform was covered with soil to prevent it from catching fire, then burning pine knots covered in fat oil were placed upon it, and it was pushed up to the top of the pole. This fire, kept burning all night, made a wide circle of light into which no Indian dared to come.

Sam Dale and the Canoe Fight

After the terrible massacre at Fort Mims, the Red Sticks began attacking plantations, settlements, and traders everywhere.

Sam Dale was sent up the Alabama River with some men to look for them and destroy them. One day, while Dale's men were divided, some on one side of the river and some on the other, they saw a flat-bottom canoe floating downstream with eleven Indians in it. The Chief had a panther skin around his head and hanging down his back! He and his men were painted and were plainly on the warpath. But there were more Red Sticks on the warpath coming up behind them through the woods.

Sam called for Caesar, a black boatman, to bring his canoe to shore. The canoe was so small that only three more men were able to get into it. These were Sam Dale, Jere Austill, and James Smith. When the Indians saw them, two jumped out of their boat to swim ashore, but Smith and Dale killed both of them. Then Dale ordered Caesar to paddle his canoe right up alongside the Indians' and hold the two canoes together. Dale and his men now fought with one foot in each boat, but as the two boats began to drift apart, Dale jumped into the Indians' boat.

Sam Dale's Canoe Fight

One after another, the Indians were killed until there were only two Red Sticks left. One was Tar-cha-chee a noted Indian wrestler. Tar-cha-chee shook himself, gave the war whoop of his tribe, and cried out, "Big Sam, I am a man! I am coming! Come on!" They fought until Tar-cha-chee was wounded. He tried to rise, crying out, "Tar-cha-chee is a man! He is not afraid to die!" Dale killed him.

There was now only one wounded Indian left. He gave the war whoop and, in tones of hatred, exclaimed, "I am a warrior! I am not afraid to die!", before he fell dead. The fight had lasted only ten minutes. Now, all the Indians began to fear Sam Dale.

In the fight, Dale and his men killed all but one of the Indians, and he fell into the water.

You must not think that Sam Dale was cruel. He tried to be a friend to the Indians, and most of them liked him. He was kind and honest. But he could not let the warriors murder the women and children and burn the towns, as Tecumseh had told them to do. Sam helped to fight them many times during the cruel Creek war.

Men like Sam Dale made good soldiers and fought bravely for their homes and families. There were good Indians, too, like the great chief Pushmataha (Push-ma-ta-ha), who liked the Americans and helped them.

Sam Dale had so many interesting stories from helping the settlers that many people enjoyed hearing him talk. The President of the United States once sent for Sam and enjoyed his stories so much that he asked him to come again. All of the best people of the day knew and loved this brave, good man.

The Creek War

At this time, many soldiers were sent into Alabama to put an end to the trouble with the Creeks. General Andrew Jackson and General John Coffee from Tennessee led these soldiers who were mostly backwoodsmen. There were many battles, but in the end, General Jackson won a great victory at Horseshoe Bend on the Tallapoosa River. The Creeks asked for peace and had to give up a great deal of their land.

Although the Indians had been badly defeated, Red Eagle had not yet been captured. No victory could satisfy General Jackson as long as Red Eagle was still in power. One day, while General Jackson was sitting in his tent planning what to do next, one of his men reported that Red Eagle wanted to see him. As Weatherford (Red Eagle) rode up, General Jackson said, "How dare you, sir, ride up to my tent after murdering the women and children of Fort Mims?"

Red Eagle replied, "I am not afraid of you, General Jackson. I fear no man. I am a Creek warrior. I have nothing to request on behalf of myself. You can kill me if you wish. I come to beg you to send for the women and children of the war party, who are starving in the woods. Their fields and cribs of corn have been destroyed by your people, who have driven them into the woods without one ear of corn. I hope you will send out a party to bring them safely here in order that they may be fed. I exerted myself to prevent the massacre of women and children at Fort Mims. I am now done fighting. The Red Sticks are nearly all dead. If I could fight you any longer, I would most heartily do so. Send for the women and children. They never did you any harm. But kill me if the white people want it done!"

There was a cry from the soldiers, "Kill him! Kill him!" General Jackson looked at Weatherford with respect and said, "A man who would kill as brave a man as this would rob the dead!"

You might be surprised to find out that after this William Weatherford settled down on his plantation and became an honored citizen. He and General Jackson became friends; and it is said that Weatherford visited General Jackson at Hermitage, General Jackson's home near Nashville.

Sam Dale's Ride

Sam Dale and Paddy

The people of the United States believed that the English had sent Tecumseh to persuade the Creek Indians to fight the whites. They were angry with the English for taking American seamen off American ships and claiming that they were English seamen; so the United States had a second war with the English.

Near the close of the war between England and the United States, it was important that a message be carried from the government in Washington to General Andrew Jackson, who was then fighting the English around New Orleans. When the message arrived at Milledgeville, Georgia, Sam Dale was selected as the best man to carry it five hundred fifty miles farther to New Orleans.

This is the way Sam Dale told the story of his ride:

"Colonel Hawkins, the Creek agent, and General McIntosh, in command of Georgia troops, urged me to take charge of the dispatches. Mounted on a compactly built horse noted for his wind and muscle, I set out the same night, taking only my blanket, my flint and steel, my pistols, and a wallet of Indian flour for myself and horse. It took almost eight days to reach General Jackson. It was after midnight before I could deliver my dispatches. The General asked if I was broken down by my rapid ride. I told him, "No!"

Holding up the dispatches, he said, "This express has been brought from Georgia in eight days. You must return to the agency as fast as you came. I will provide you with a good horse. In an hour you will be given your papers."

"And what," I asked, 'is to be done with Paddy?"

"Who is Paddy, sir?"

"The pony, General, that brought me from Georgia!"

"You don't mean to say, sir, that you rode one horse all the way from Georgia in seven and one-half days?"

"I mean nothing less, General."

"Then, sir, he won't be able to go back."

"He's like myself, General, very tough."

"Now tell me, how far can you ride that horse a day?"

"Seventy or eighty miles a day with light weight."

"Light weight?"

"Yes, sir, an empty belly and no saddle bags."

"Well, major, that will do."

"I set off at daylight; and, after crossing the lake, I met an officer who demanded knowing where I was from."

"Headquarters," I replied.

"Well, you must stop and tell me the news."

"I can't stop. If you want news you must travel my way."

"Sir you don't know me. I am Colonel Sparks of the United States army. You must stop."

"And I, sir, am Major Samuel Dale; and, when I am under orders, I stop for no man."

The colonel bit his lip but wheeled and rode with me several miles. When parting, I asked him whether I was right or wrong in refusing to halt.

"Right, Major, and I ask your pardon."

On the third day, I reached Mobile, and at night on the eighth, I stopped at Fort Decatur on the Tallapoosa. The trip had been very hard. The weather was cold, the streams swollen; and some nights I had to sleep outdoors. The night I reached Fort Decatur, I was so cold and stiff that I had to be helped off my horse. I was given some hot coffee, and then the officers crowded around to learn of General Jackson's victory at New Orleans. You should have heard them cheer."

The Indians admired Dale for his courage.

A Choctaw chief, standing at Dale's grave, said, "You sleep here, Sam Tholocco; but your spirit is a chieftain and a brave in the hunting ground of the sky."

CHAPTER 6
STATEHOOD

Alabama's Creed

I believe in Alabama, a state dedicated to a faith in God and the enlightenment of mankind; to a democracy that safeguards the liberties of each citizen and to the conservation of her youth, her ideals, and her soil. I believe it is my duty to obey her laws, to respect her flag and to be alert to her needs and generous in my efforts to foster her advancement within the statehood of the world.

Vocabulary:

Territory	Symbol	Shilling
Patriotism	Seal	Governor
Vehicle	Vestibule	Two bits
Horse block	Dinner	Brocade
Hitching post	Amen	Barter
Six bits		

Copywork:

The Alabama Creed (above)

Research Suggestions:

1. What events occurred for Mobile to become part of Alabama?

2. Who was the first Governor of Alabama? Write a short essay about his life in your *Alabama Timeline Journal Notebook*.

3. Find out who each one of our governors have been, add each one of them to the *Alabama*

Timeline Journal Notebook under the date they were sworn into office.

4. What is our state bird? Add your research into the *Alabama Timeline Journal Notebook*. When did the state officially claim our state bird?

5. What is our state flower? Add your research into your *Alabama Timeline Journal Notebook*. Why was this flower chosen as the state flower? When did the state make the choice to have this flower?

6. Research the history of Alabama's state flag.

7. What are the four cities or towns that have been Alabama's capitol? Add them into your *Alabama Timeline Journal Notebook* under the dates that each one became the capitol.

8. At the time of statehood, how many different territories and countries had claimed Alabama? What is the State Seal? How many state seals has Alabama had? Who designed our first state seal? What does our current seal look like?

People & Places to Research:

Isaac Smith	James Jackson	General John Coffee
William Watt Bibb	Ferdinand Sanonner	General Lafayette
Governor Pickens	Chief Doublehead	William Bibb
Treaty of Fort Jackson	George Colbert	Levi Colbert
Alabama Territory	Mississippi Territory	Louisiana Territory

Science & Nature Study:

Southern Pine	Camellia	Cotton
Northern Red Oak	Tornado	Water Oak
Meteorologist	Shumard Oak	

Project Suggestions:

1. Draw our state flag in your *Alabama Timeline Journal Notebook*.

2. Plan an event to celebrate Alabama's birthday.

3. How old is the state of Alabama?

4. Draw a picture of the state seal.

5. Draw a picture of the state bird.

6. Draw a picture of the state flower.

Map Work:

1. Mark & label all the different state capitols on your map. What year did each one become the capitol? Why do you think these towns were chosen as the capitols? Why have we had so many capitols? Add your answers to your *Alabama Timeline Journal Notebook*.

St. Stephen	Tuscaloosa	Cahaba
Huntsville	Montgomery	

2. Put Fort Mims on the map.

Field Trip Suggestions:

1. Visit the capitol at Montgomery.

2. Visit one of Alabama's universities. Call ahead and schedule a history tour.

Alabama Becomes Part of the United States

Not long after the English took Louisiana from the French, the English colonies in America grew dissatisfied with the way England, "the Mother Country" as they called her, was treating them. England and the colonies quarreled for about twelve years, and then they began to fight.

On July 4, 1776, the English colonies said that they were "free and independent states" and named themselves "The United States of America."

Although the colonies said they were free, our colonial forefathers, had to fight for eight long years before England would agree to give us up as an independent country. We call this long struggle, "The Revolutionary War".

In this war General George Washington was our commander-in-chief. He fought and planned well for us to gain our independence.

What was done with Alabama after the Revolutionary War? The northern part of Alabama continued as part of Georgia. But Mobile, in the southern part of Alabama, was given to Spain by England, and a Spanish flag was flown over the fort in Mobile.

The United States was dissatisfied that Mobile was not part of The United States of America. But the French then regained control of Mobile. We then reclaimed Mobile as part of the negotiations in 1803 as part of the Louisiana Purchase.

Timeline

December 6, 1816
Montgomery County, Alabama established, being named in honor of Lemuel P. Montgomery, military officer killed in the battle of Horseshoe Bend.

1816
The Alabama Republican Newspaper is established in Huntsville, Alabama.

1817-1825
James Monroe is elected President of the United States.

1817
Alabama becomes a territory when congress passes the enabling act allowing Mississippi to become a state.

Alabama Becomes a State

As you have learned, Alabama has been both part of what was at one time considered to be part of the Georgia and Louisiana Territories.

Alabama then became part of the Mississippi Territory, which was divided out of the Louisiana Territory. In 1817, after much discussion that followed the Creek War, the Mississippi Territory was divided. The western half was still called Mississippi, but the eastern half was named Alabama Territory, after the Alabama Indians. On December 14, 1819, Alabama became a state. That is why we call December 14 Alabama's birthday!

Before the Mississippi Territory was divided, there were many different suggestions on how to divide Mississippi and Alabama up into two different states or territories. Many people had concerns about some of the proposals.

The suggestion that caused the most concern was to divide the Mississippi Territory East to West giving the lower half to Mississippi. This would have made the city Mobile, a Mississippi town. Alabama would not have had the Mobile Bay. This would have significantly changed the economic situation for what was to be the new territory of Alabama. The Mobile Bay has always proven to be a great source of export and import for the state of Alabama and the entire south.

Sam Dale had been appointed to the committee that divided the Mississippi territory creating the state of Mississippi and the Alabama Territory. Sam was once again an integral part of the history of the State of Alabama, fighting for the territory to be divided, giving Mississippi and Alabama each access to international water ways through the Gulf of Mexico.

Timeline

1817
Cherokee and Chickasaw give up most of their land south of the Tennessee River.

1817
French arrive in Marengo County starting the Vine & Olive Colony.

1817
Alabama becomes the territory of Alabama with St. Stephen as the capitol.

1817-1819
St. Stephen was the capitol of the Mississippi territory. Once Alabama was a separate territory, St. Stephen then became the capital of the Alabama Territory.

From Territory to Statehood

There are many differences between a territory and state, but we will mention only two of them. There were two main reasons for the people of Alabama to desire statehood.

When Alabama was a territory instead of a state, the United States could tell Alabama as a territory when its laws must be changed; a state has more control over the changing or making of laws.

Another difference is the President of the United States appoints the governor of a territory; a state elects its own governor.

Of course, Alabama was excited to become a state electing its leaders and voting on laws.

Alabama's first governor was William Watt Bibb. He had been appointed governor of Alabama Territory and the people liked him enough to elect him first governor of the state.

State Seal

> **Timeline**
>
> **January 19, 1818**
> First legislature of the Alabama Territory convened at a hotel in St. Stephen, the territorial capital.
>
> **February 6, 1818**
> Lawrence County, Alabama established and named in honor of J. Lawrence of the U.S. Navy.
>
> **February 6, 1818**
> Marengo County, Alabama established and named in honor of an Italian Battlefield in Italy near Turin.
>
> **February 6, 1818**
> Franklin County, Alabama established and named in honor of Benjamin Franklin.

Every state has a seal which is put on all the state laws. Stamping its seal on a paper is the state's way of signing its name. After the War Between the States, some people who had never lived in Alabama were in leadership of the state. At this time, the seal was changed and our second state seal was selected.

In 1939, there was a bill introduced to the state legislation to change our seal to what we currently have, which is our third seal.

Alabama's State Song

You have studied Alabama's seal, the state bird, the state flower, and the state flag. Now we will learn about Alabama's state song. Select the stanzas you like the most, salute the flag, and sing them.

Alabama

Alabama, Alabama
We will aye be true to thee,
From thy Southern shores where growth.
By the sea thy orange tree
To thy Northern vale where flowth,
Deep blue the Tennessee
Alabama, Alabama, we will aye be true to thee.
Broad thy stream whose name thou bearest,
Grand thy Bigbee rolls along
Fair thy Coosa-Tallapoosa,
Bold thy Warrior dark and strong.
Goodlier than the land that Moses
Climbed lone Nebb's Mount to see.
Alabama, Alabama, we will aye be true to thee.
Brave and pure thy men and women,
Better this than corn and wine
Make us worthy, God in Heaven
Of this goodly land of Thine.
Hearts as open as thy doorways.
Liberal hands and spirits free.
Alabama, Alabama, we will aye be true to thee.
Little, little can I give thee,
Alabama, mother mine.
But that little - hand, brain, spirit.

Timeline

February 6, 1818
Tuscaloosa County, Alabama established and named in honor of Choctaw Chief Tuscaloosa.

February 6, 1818
Lauderdale County, Alabama is established, being named in honor of Colonel James Lauderdale of Tennessee.

February 6, 1818
Blount County, Alabama is established, being named in honor of Willie G. Blount, a Governor in Tennessee.

February 6, 1818
Limestone County, Alabama is established, being named for the vast amount of limestone found in the rich soil.

> All I have and am are thine.
> Take, O take, the gift and giver.
> Take and serve thyself with me.
> Alabama, Alabama, we will aye be true to thee.

The state song, *Alabama*, was written by Miss Julia Tutwiler.

Alabama's Capitols

A state must have a capitol city where the laws are made and the governor resides. Alabama has had five capitols. St. Stephens on the Tombigbee River was the capitol of Alabama territory and the first state capitol.

At one time, St. Stephen's was a busy place. The town grew and in 1811, an academy was opened. People moved in and built comfortable homes. When Alabama became a territory in 1817, St. Stephens was the capitol of Alabama Territory, and served as the first state capital for a few short months.

Once the capitol was moved from St. Stephen, the people began to move away until it was entirely deserted, with nothing to tell of its past life except an old cemetery and some stone foundations of the old buildings.

The second capitol of Alabama was located in Huntsville. Soon after Alabama became a state, Huntsville was chosen as the place to meet to draw up a plan of government. Huntsville is named as Alabama's second capitol.

There is a wonderful spring in the heart of the city of Huntsville that gushes into a large stream. The story is told that a man named John Hunt, having heard of the spring, made up his mind to find the spring and live near it. He asked the Indians for directions to

---

Timeline

February 7, 1818
Cahawba County, Alabama established, being named for the Cahaba River. It was later renamed to Bibb County, Alabama.

February 7, 1818
Shelby County, Alabama established, being named for Kentucky Governor, Isaac Shelby.

February 8, 1818
Cotaco County, Alabama was established. It was later to be renamed Morgan County.

February 9, 1818
Dallas County, Alabama is established and named in honor of U.S. Secretary of the Treasury, Alexander J. Dallas.

> **Timeline**
>
> **February 13, 1818**
> Marion County, Alabama is established, being named in honor of American Revolutionary General from South Carolina, Francis Marion.
>
> **February 13, 1818**
> Conecuh County, Alabama is established, being named in honor of the Native American words for "Land of Cane."
>
> **November 20, 1818**
> St. Clair County, Alabama is established, being named in honor of General Arthur St. Clair, 9th President of the Continental Congress.
>
> **November 21, 1818**
> Autauga County, Alabama is established, being named for the Autauga Indian tribe that made this area their home.

the spring and built his cabin nearby. Other people begin to hear of this lovely place and built there also. By 1819, Huntsville was a village with comfortable homes and many families.

Huntsville would have been a good town for the capitol except for its location. Because it was located in the northeastern part of the state and far away from the middle and southern part, where most of the people lived at the time; it was decided to build a capitol where the Cahaba River flows into the Alabama River and name the town Cahaba.

Cahaba was near the middle of the state and easy to get to by river and by road. It had an excellent overflowing well which would give a plentiful supply of healthy water. Many people moved to Cahaba, but during the long rainy seasons, the Alabama and Cahaba Rivers would rise and flood the town. The streets would become streams; the yards and even the first floors of the houses would be covered with water. The governor had to go to the capitol building in a canoe. Of course, this would not work, so it was decided to move the capitol to Tuscaloosa.

Tuscaloosa was well laid out, with three rows of great oak trees, one row on each side of the street and one row down the middle of the wide streets. The streets were lined with comfortable homes; lovely flower gardens transformed Tuscaloosa into the picture of a perfect park. The state university was established there. The people of Tuscaloosa were very proud of their town.

In 1836, while Tuscaloosa was the capitol of Alabama, the Native American Indians of Alabama were moved west to what was then called Indian Territory, now the state of Oklahoma. A few words taken from a speech said to have been made by an Indian chief to the legislature of Alabama illustrates how the Natives felt about giving up their homeland. This is a translation of what the chief said:

"I come, brothers, to see the great house of Alabama and the men that make the laws, and to say farewell in brotherly kindness before I go to the far west…In these lands of Alabama, which have belonged to my forefathers, and where their bones lie buried, I see that the Indian fires are going out. New fires are lighting in the west and we are going there. I leave the graves of my fathers but the Indian fires are going out, almost clean gone and new fires are lighting there for us."

After several years of discussion and debate it was decided to move the capitol of Alabama to Montgomery. There were many people disappointed because of the change in the location of the capitol, but it was the logical choice because Montgomery was more centrally located in the state, making it easier for everyone to access the capitol city.

> ### Timeline
>
> **November 21, 1818**
> Cahaba is designated by the territorial legislation as Alabama State capitol. Huntsville served as the temporary capitol as the capitol in Cahaba was being built.
>
> **1818**
> Florence, Alabama is surveyed by an Italian engineer.
>
> **1818-1820**
> Dred Scott the slave whose name was associated with the Dred Scott Court case was in Madison and Lauderdale counties with the Peter Blow family. He was later sold to Dr. John Emerson. It was at this time that Scott made his fight for freedom.

Our Capitol, Montgomery

Montgomery is on the Alabama River, just below where the Coosa and the Tallapoosa join to form the Alabama. It is not many miles from where old Fort Toulouse was located. Andrew Dexter, one of the earliest settlers, wanted Montgomery to become the capitol of Alabama and the capitol building to be on Goat Hill. It looked for a long time as if Andrew Dexter's dream for the capitol was never going to happen—but in 1847 Montgomery became the capitol.

THE "YELLOW-HAMMERS"

How did we become the Yellow-hammer State? You have read about some of the interesting things found in the mounds the Indians left in Alabama. Among these are vases, dishes,

> **Timeline**
>
> **1819**
> The capital was moved from St. Stephen to Huntsville.
>
> **March 2, 1819**
> President Monroe signed the Alabama enabling act.
>
> **July 5 – August 2, 1819**
> Constitutional Convention meets in Huntsville and adopts state constitution.
>
> **Sept. 20-21, 1819**
> First general election is held as specified by the state constitution.
>
> **Oct.-Dec. 1819**
> Alabama State General Assembly meets in Huntsville while the capitol was being built in Cahaba.

and knives. Some of the dishes and vases have pictures of birds carved or painted on them. The birds in the pictures are large and strong like our woodpeckers. Could the woodpecker have been a sacred bird to the Indians? We do know why some men who lived in Alabama later wore a feather from a bird belonging to the woodpecker family.

Many of the people living in the state tried to do something for the South during the time period known as the Civil War. The men fought while the women stayed at home and cared for their families and helped provide for the army.

These brave women hoed the cotton, gathered it, spun it into cloth, and made clothes for our troops. There was no money to buy anything, even if there had been anything to sell. There was no money in the South.

The soldiers wore their uniforms to rags, since there was no woolen cloth to make new ones. The women wove heavy cloth of cotton and made uniforms for the soldiers.

In those days, men wore coats with two long tails to them. The women made these tails on the uniform coats. The greatest trouble was that the uniforms were nearly white and the enemy could see them at long distances. The women had no dye, but someone remembered a dye the Indians had taught the first settlers to make.

Bark from a tree was boiled to make a dye. When the uniforms were dipped in it, they turned yellow. One day a company of soldiers marched away, feeling much better in their bright new uniforms. Someone standing near said, "They look like yellow-hammers."

Do you know what a "yellow-hammer" is? Perhaps you know it by its real name, which is flicker. This bright, beautiful bird has lived in our state as long as anyone can remember. Even De Soto and his men must have seen it when they marched through the state.

The flicker belongs to the woodpecker family. This handsome bird has golden wings, a white spot where the tail joins the body, and a brilliant red head. Think of what, the first settlers must have thought, when they heard the "drum" sound as he peck-pecked away on a hollow log. He has the strong bill of the woodpecker family to do his drumming.

Often the Confederate soldiers from Alabama stuck a bright yellow feather from this bird in their hats. They liked being called "Yellow-Hammers." Above the Confederate flag, they sometimes carried a stuffed yellowhammer. The red and gold of the Yellowhammer was a cheerful sight for the eyes of the soldiers. When the time came to choose a state bird, this is why the yellowhammer was chosen.

CHAPTER 7
INDIAN REMOVAL

Vocabulary:

Territory	Interrupt	Treaty
Victory	Communicate	Eviction
Economically	Inhabitant	Stockade
Acre	Surrender	Lieutenant
Imagine	Cleansing	Language

Research Suggestions:

1. Research the history of the Choctaw Indians and their removal treaties. What events occurred during the negotiations of treaties? Who were some of the interesting chiefs in the Choctaw Nations? Add your discoveries to your *Alabama Timeline Journal Notebook*.

2. Research the history of the Chickasaw Indians and their removal treaties. What interesting event occurred during their negotiations? Who were some of the interesting people involved? How did they help or hurt the negotiations of treaties? Add your discoveries to your *Alabama Timeline Journal Notebook*.

3. Research the history of the Cherokee Indians. What are some of the interesting events that occurred during the removal treaties? Add your discoveries to your *Alabama Timeline Journal Notebook*.

4. What is the total number of Native Americans that were relocated? How many died because of the long journey they had to endure during the removal from their homelands? Now use these numbers to come up with a death percentage because of relocation. Add your discoveries to your *Alabama Timeline Journal Notebook*.

5. How many years did it take the government to take over all the native territories in the East?

Add your discoveries to your *Alabama Timeline Journal Notebook*.

6. Who was Sequoyah? What tribal nation was he from? What special things did he do for his people? Where did he die? Add your discoveries to your *Alabama Timeline Journal Notebook*.

People & Places to Research:

Sequoyah	Fort Payne	George Gist (or Guess) Chief
Doublehead	Chief George Colbert	Levi Colbert
Captain John D. Chisholm	James Logan Colbert	Colonel A.M. Upshaw
Chief John Ross	Chief Tuscumbia	Rachel Jackson
Colonel Return J. Meigs		

Science & Nature Study:

Holly	Blackjack Oak	Sassafras
Southern Red Oak	Cherry bark Oak	

Project Suggestions:

If you were to walk from Chattanooga, Tennessee to Oklahoma City, Oklahoma, how many miles would you travel on your journey? Approximately how long would it take?

Map Work:

1. You should have already labeled the Native American territories on your map. Now add the Trail of Tears to your map in the *Alabama Timeline Journal Notebook*.

2. Find Dekalb County, mark and label it on your map in your *Alabama Timeline Journal Notebook*.

Local & Family History:

Go to your local library's genealogy room and look up information about your city/county and family. Call your grandparents and older family members to learn what you can about the family.

1. How did your city or town get its name? Who was it named after? What year was it founded or incorporated? Add this information to your *Alabama Timeline Journal Notebook*.

> ### Timeline
>
> **October 28, 1819**
> Alabama State Legislature elects William Rufus King and John W. Walker the first U.S. Senators for Alabama.
>
> **December 13, 1819**
> Jackson County, Alabama was established, named in honor of General Andrew Jackson. Jackson became U.S. President 10 years later.
>
> **December 13, 1819**
> Perry County, Alabama was established, being named in honor of Oliver Hazard Perry of Rhode Island and U.S. Navy.
>
> **December 13, 1819**
> Jefferson County, Alabama was established, being named in honor of Thomas Jefferson.
>
> **December 14, 1819**
> Alabama entered the union as the 22nd state of the U.S.

Scottish History in Alabama

The Scottish history in Alabama is exceedingly rich. You must remember that the first traders to bring mule trains into Alabama were Scottish. Many of the traders lived with the Natives. Having homes in the native towns, they typically married native women, raising a happy family together. Many of these Scottish men were warmly welcomed into the native families, often being elevated to leadership amongst the family. These marriages were common and also good for relations between the two cultures. It is important to understand, however, that when the removal of the Native Americans occurred, a large percentage of the people that were displaced had no more Native blood in their veins than many of us. Many of the people who moved westward were as little as one-sixth Native American and had a much stronger Celtic heritage.

Chief Doublehead

Doublehead was one of Alabama's many remarkable chiefs. History has not remembered him as well as some of the chiefs of Alabama, although he was from a prominent Cherokee family. His life and family played a huge role, not only in the history of Alabama, but also in the rest of the country. Chief Doublehead's sister was the mother of Sequoya, the creator of the Cherokee written language. This makes Doublehead an uncle to one of the most famous Native Americans in history. Two of Doublehead's daughters were wives to Chief George Colbert. These marriages strongly linked the Cherokee to the Chickasaw in Alabama. Chief Doublehead, unlike most of his relations, was greatly feared throughout the Tennessee River Valley.

Doublehead was a successful business man, but only a secondary chief among the Cherokee nation until the death of his brother Old Tassel in 1788. Old Tassel was murdered by a young settler who felt he was avenging the death of his parents who were killed by a Cherokee raiding party. Old Tassel had come to talk with some government authorities under a flag of truce. The door was guarded, keeping his warriors out while the unarmed chief was murdered. After his death, Doublehead began to ascend to leadership.

Doublehead took a war party up through Tennessee, scalping and murdering to retaliate for Old Tassel's death. After he felt the death had been avenged, he settled down and began to use the authority given him to influence the treaties that were negotiated with the U.S. government for the Cherokee nation. It was only a matter of time before Doublehead was killed. His murderer was actually another chief that felt Doublehead had handled some government negations more for his own personal gain than for the best interest of the Cherokee tribe.

Sequoya

Sequoya was born in 1776 to Wut-teh (sister of Chief Doublehead) and Nathaniel Gist. His father was a fur trader and his mother the daughter of a Cherokee Chief. There is a possibility he was born handicapped. Sequoya in Cherokee means "pig's foot." Handicapped or not, Sequoya led a very fascinating life. His own people thought he was crazy until he finished his language or "talking leaves."

Timeline

1819- 1820
William Bibb was appointed the Governor of the territory of Alabama. He died in office.

1819
A large band of Cherokee left Alabama and went to Texas, receiving a land grant from the Mexican Government.

1819-1825
The Capital is moved from Huntsville to Cahaba.

1820
Alabama Census of the Alabama Population: 144,317
White Population: 96,245
African-American: 48,082
Slave population: 47,449
Free African-American: 633

1820
Bibb County, Alabama is established when Cahawba County, Alabama was renamed to Bibb County, Alabama in honor of William W. Bibb the first governor of Alabama.

> **Timeline**
>
> **May 8, 1820**
> The Alabama Supreme Court convenes for the first time.
>
> **July 10, 1820**
> Governor William Bibb dies from a riding injury.
>
> **July 10, 1820**
> Thomas Bibb, president of the state senate becomes governor after William Bibb's death, as required by the state constitution. He served from 1820-1821.
>
> **October 22, 1820**
> The first steamboat reaches Montgomery from Mobile, opening river boat trade through the Alabama River.
>
> **December 20, 1820**
> Pickens County, Alabama is established, being named in honor of General Andrew Pickens.

Sequoya lived for years in what is now known as Dekalb County, Alabama. It took many years of his life to develop the Cherokee language. Having the written language helped the Cherokee communicate with family and friends in other areas. This gave them somewhat of an advantage over other tribes. The Cherokee published a newspaper called "The Cherokee Phoenix." Until the development of the Cherokee language, the Creek were the most powerful tribe in Alabama. However, the Cherokee could now be educated in their own language. But even with their education, they could not evade the removal that the United States government demanded.

The Native Indian Removal

The Trail of Tears is one of the most heartrending incidents in our country's history. About one-third of the people that began the journey died before reaching the new lands. They were not given time to plan for the journey or the weather changes. They were forced to travel and at the mercy of the federal troops to have food rations at different stopping points, only to find that much of the food was spoiled. As a result, the weak, sick, young and old are the ones that paid with their lives. Most of the deaths involved infants, children, and the elderly. This added to the many reasons the Native Americans had no faith in the United States Government's promises.

Indian Removal Treaties

When Andrew Jackson led the U.S. military to victory at Horseshoe Bend, the Creek Nation surrendered 22,000,000 acres (this included over half of the territory of Alabama) to the government. This made it possible for Alabama to become the 22nd state added into the Union. This was also the beginning of the end of the life that the Indian nations of Alabama had always known. Andrew Jackson's victory at Horseshoe Bend and again at New Orleans positioned him to become our 7th president in March of 1829. President Jackson signed more than 90 removal treaties during his term as president. Most of Jackson's treaties were broken before he left the office of president in 1837. About 100,000,000 acres from Illinois to Florida were taken from the Indian nations under his leadership. The territory replacing the Indians lands was only a little over 30,000,000 acres. Most of it was in what later became the state of Oklahoma.

The year of 1814 was a time of great excitement! Everyone was moving west; Alabama was 'the west' at this time. Many of the Creek peoples left Alabama when the Treaty of 1814 was signed. Once statehood was established in 1819, the planters began to arrive with great dreams of wonderful crops on rich Alabama soil. This made the Native American removal more economically and politically urgent. The Creek removal was signed in 1820, finishing the evacuation of the Creek. By 1827, the only trace of the Creek people in Alabama were the people that denied their heritage to avoid leaving their homes. Settlers moving into the state did not realize the other half of the state was still being occupied by the Cherokee, Choctaw, and Chickasaw peoples. These tribes were unwilling to give up their homes to the white settlers. The removal treaties, however, continued to be signed to drive them from their homes.

> **Timeline**
>
> **1820**
> President Monroe reserves a site for a town to be called Decatur, honoring Commodore Decatur of the U.S. Navy.
>
> **1821**
> Thomas Bibb is the governor of the state of Alabama.
>
> **1821**
> Morgan County, Alabama is established when Cotaco County, Alabama is renamed.
>
> **December 17, 1821**
> Covington County, Alabama is established, being named in honor of Brigadier General Leonard Covington.
>
> **December 17, 1821**
> Pike County, Alabama is established, being named in honor of Zebulon Pike, of New Jersey. Pike is the explorer who led the expedition to Southern Colorado discovering Pikes Peak.

Timeline

1821
Senator Edmund Winston Pettus was born in Limestone County, Alabama.

1821-1825
Israel Pickens is the Governor of the state of Alabama.

1822
The steamboat, "Rocket" begins regular passage from Muscle Shoals to the mouth of the Tennessee River at the Ohio River.

1822
The State's first female academy is opened in Athens. It later becomes Athens State University. It is currently the oldest school in Alabama.

December 26, 1823
Walker County, Alabama is established, being named for John W. Walker, U.S. Senator.

The Choctaw were the next to feel the pressure of the treaties. By May of 1830, the Choctaw treaty was signed giving the U.S. Government 13,000,000 acres of Choctaw territory in exchange for land in what is now the state of Arkansas. There was a second group of Choctaw removed from the Mississippi area to what is now the state of Oklahoma in 1842. The rest of the Choctaw had already been pushed from Arkansas into Oklahoma by 1842.

The Cherokee and Chickasaw were more determined to keep the land of their grandfathers. The government had much more difficulty negotiating with these tribes. By the 1820's, the Cherokee nations had established a formal government. Then the removal treaty was signed in 1835, surrendering all Cherokee territory east of the Mississippi for 5,000,000 dollars and land in the new Indian Territory. Only a few hundred Cherokee were present and 20 signed the treaty. None of the twenty were part of the Cherokee governing council. This caused major division in the Cherokee nation. Over 15,000 Cherokees protested the treaty. Many did not believe the government would remove the Cherokee. They stayed in their homes, not expecting the government to become so shockingly aggressive.

The way in which these people were taken from their homes was a heartbreaking event. Imagine what it might be like if soldier came to your home to move you and your family to another area. Many children were separated from their parents, husbands from their wives. They were removed from their homes with only the things they could carry with them. They were then taken to stockades where they were put in pens, something like the holding pens for the cattle, at the stock auction. Many were numbered and chained like animals, making it easier to control them.

The Chickasaw began to negotiate a treaty with the aggressive U.S. government in January of 1832. The government wanted the Chickasaws to move to Choctaw land. But the Chickasaw did not feel this would be a suitable situation.

Chief Levi Colbert addressed the President of the United States, saying the Chickasaw people were not ready to migrate and that the treaty was not valid. He said the land "...which the Choctaw perhaps will let us have, is most of it big prairies, mighty little wood, water, or good land; it will be mighty hard for my people to live there... it was the words in your message which alarmed and roused the fears of my people; you speak of this treaty as final, this is not the sense of it; we have not got as yet any home in the west... you can see the strong and marked difference of our condition here and in the wild distant regions of the west, surrounded by none but distance and deer trade and warlike tribes thrown together."

Chief Colbert understood what a difficult time the tribes would have living together after so many years of war and revelry. Several years of negotiating passed before the Chickasaw began their journey to a new territory in June of 1837. It was January of 1838 before they arrived in the new territory.

> **Timeline**
>
> **1824**
> The State Bank is established in Cahaba.
>
> **1824**
> William Weatherford (Red Eagle) dies at his plantation home in Baldwin County, located on the Little River.
>
> **1824**
> John Tyler Morgan, future senator of Alabama, was born in Athens, Tennessee.
>
> **December 20, 1824**
> Fayette County, Alabama is established, being named in honor of Marquis de Lafayette, who fought for U.S. freedom from the British in the American Revolutionary War.
>
> **December 22, 1824**
> Dale County, Alabama is established, being named in honor of General Sam Dale.

CHAPTER 8
EARLY LIFE ON ALABAMA PLANTATIONS

Vocabulary:

Bandannas	Calico	Cottonade
Physician	Revival	Tender
Granny	Mutton	Tallow
Forge	Bellows	Anvil
Sidesaddle	Horse block	Gorgeous
Haughty	Escort	

People & Place to Research:

Andrew Jackson Beard	Robert McCorstine	Justice John McKinley
Daniel Pratt	Howard Weeden	Governor Robert Miller Patton

Research Suggestions:

1. When was the first cotton gin built in Alabama? Where was it built? Who invented the cotton gin? Add your research to your *Alabama Timeline Journal Notebook*.

2. Who invented matches? Add your research to your *Alabama Timeline Journal Notebook*.

3. Who invented the sewing machine? Add your research to your *Alabama Timeline Journal Notebook*.

Science & Nature Study:

Wild Geranium	Wild Ginger	Feverwort
Trout Lily	Thimbleweed	Hoar-hound
Mullein	Burdock	Elderberries
Mint	Chamomile	Lavender
Tansy	Cotton	

Project Suggestions:

1. Sing some of the revival songs.

2. Make soap and/or candles.

3. Build a flower and herb garden of native Alabama plants.

Field Trip Suggestions:

1. Village or re-enactment that has a blacksmith at work, as well as candle and soap making.

2. Visit a Cotton Gin.

Local & Family History:

Go to your local library's genealogy room and look up information about your city/county and family. Call your grandparents and older family members to learn what you can about the family.

1. What was the first church in your town? Is the congregation still meeting? If so, visit the building. There is probably a person in the congregation that could give you the history of the building & church. Add this information to your *Alabama Timeline Journal Notebook*.

Timeline

1825-1829
John Quincy Adams is President of the United States.

1825-1829
John Murphy is the governor of the state of Alabama.

1826-1846
The capital is moved from Cahaba to Tuscaloosa.

June 1, 1826
Amelia Gayle Gorgas was born Greensboro, Alabama.

1829-1831
Gabriel Moore is the governor of the state of Alabama.

1829-1837
Andrew Jackson is President of the United States.

Plantation Life

The mystical Old South has always been presented in movie and books as a fairytale. After the native people of Alabama were removed, planters began to flood into Alabama for the rich land that was now available. The land was planted in acre after acre of cotton. To maintain the level of work needed to complete the production of cotton on a plantation, workers were in high demand. Slavery was the labor force that maintained these plantations. Have you ever wondered what the lifestyle might be like on the plantation? This might give you a little glimpse into the lives of the slaves.

Slave Life on a Plantation

Slavery is still practiced in many parts of the world, but is against the law in the United States of America. It was a common practice until the Emancipative Proclamation on Jan. 1, 1863. There were many mean slave owners as well as kind slave owners. But who would want to be owned? Even if the person that owned them was kind? We are going to look at a few of the situations that *could* have happened on the plantation from a slave's perspective.

The slaves on a plantation had to work hard, but they received no pay for their work. They were considered property of the plantation. Their owner did not have to pay them for the work they performed on the plantation.

There were many different things that could occur on a plantation when a slave was disrespectful to a white person. Whipping was a punishment that most southern owners thought proper at that time. If the master's children were naughty, they expected a whipping. If they misbehaved at school or did not learn their lessons, they expected and received a whipping. Many towns had whipping posts at which law-breakers were whipped. Therefore, as a matter of course, if a slave was mouthy, lazy, or stubborn, he too, was whipped. If he took someone else's chickens, eggs, or watermelons, he would be whipped. But these whippings were not like the whippings children received—they were vastly different. The slave's whipping was given with a whip, something similar to what is used on a farm animal. The flesh on the slave's back was often ripped open by this harsh punishment. The slave, more often than not, developed an infection which could result in death.

If the slave fought or caused trouble among the other slaves, he might be shut up in a cabin by himself, with food withheld until he behaved. The slaves hated this punishment because of the loneliness and hunger.

If a slave was dangerous and very hard to manage, he might be sold to the next slave trader that came by. This meant that he would be taken far away and sold to anyone who might want to buy him. Slaves dreaded being "sold down south" or "sold down the river," as it was called. Neither the master nor the slave wanted this to happen and most planters prided themselves on never selling one of their people. Imagine what it might be like if you were sold away from your family and friends. No one should ever have to worry about themselves or family members being sold.

> **Timeline**
>
> **1830**
> Alabama Census of the Alabama Population: 309,527
> White Population: 190,406
> African-American: 119,121
> Slave Population: 117,549
> Free Black Population: 1,572
>
> **1830**
> The Choctaw & Chickasaw were being removed further west.
>
> **January 20, 1830**
> Lowndes County, Alabama is established, being named in honor of U.S. Congressman of South Carolina, William Lowndes.
>
> **September 27, 1830**
> Treaty of the Dancing Rabbit Creek was signed with the Choctaw surrendering 11 million acres to U.S. government.

The slaves did not like the overseer to come around during the night to be sure that every cabin was quiet and that nobody was moving about the quarters.

They were never allowed to leave the plantation without a written pass telling who they were, who their master was, and where they were going. There were patrols, or as the

> **Timeline**
>
> **1830**
> The Methodist church establishes LaGrange College in Colbert County.
>
> **1831**
> The first railroad west of the Allegheny Mountain is built in Tuscumbia; it runs two miles to the Tennessee River.
>
> **April 13, 1831**
> The University of Alabama is established and opens its doors to the first students.
>
> **1831-1831**
> Samuel Moore is the governor of the state of Alabama.
>
> **1831-1835**
> John Gayle is the governor of the state of Alabama.

slaves called them, "patrollers." They would arrest slaves who were on the road without a pass.

One of a slave's greatest dilemmas was the fear that when their master died, they might be given to different heirs or sold and separated from their family and friends. They were affectionate, dependable people and if treated kindly, they often loved and looked up to their "white folks." They loved their children and fellow slaves; the plantation was their home. A good master understood how his people felt, and considered it his duty to take care of them even after his death.

Christmas at the Big House

Everybody on the plantation looked forward to Christmas, just as we do today. All work was stopped Christmas Eve. The big house was decorated with holly, mistletoe, and Southern smilax. Extra-big logs burned in the great fireplaces. Everybody hung up stockings and in the morning, every stocking had a silver dime in the toe and was filled with plenty of candy, raisins, and an orange.

The fires were made early Christmas morning. Mammy was awakened before daylight by the youngsters clamoring to get up. The maids and men servants (slaves) were sure to get the white folks a Christmas gift, knowing that there was something hidden away for them.

Breakfast was better than usual, with fruit, hot waffles, sausage, and other good things. The presents were on or around a Christmas tree in the parlor, but no one could see them until after breakfast. Then everyone went into the parlor, which was bright with a roaring wood fire. There were dolls and tea sets for the girls, and wagons and tool chests for the boys, and books for all of them. Mammy got a fine bandanna and ten dollars, and each of the other house servants received a present and five dollars.

Then everybody scattered about, the children to play with their presents, mother to talk to the cook and butler about Christmas dinner, and father to look after his horses.

Christmas dinner was served on a long table covered with a fine tablecloth, beautiful china, glistening glass, and highly polished silver. The table was lighted by silver candlesticks holding tall wax candles. A roasted ham was at one end and a stuffed turkey at the other.

One dessert that was served was boiled custard served hot in covered cups. There were cakes of all kinds and a blazing plum pudding was brought in just when everyone thought he could eat no more.

There was always company for dinner. Therefore, after dinner the grown people played the piano, sang, and danced. The children could either play in the nursery or stay in the parlor with the grownups. To stay in the parlor was quite a privilege.

Christmas at the Quarters

The quarter slaves (field slaves) were not forgotten at Christmas. They cooked chickens for Christmas dinner, made cakes with icing out of the extra flour and sugar given to them, pulled sorghum candy to put into the children's stockings, and had a happy holiday.

When the plantation bell rang Christmas morning, all the slaves, both big and small, came to the big house to greet the master. Everybody had on clean clothes, had combed his hair, and was all "fixed up" for Christmas. Often, the master gave the head of each

> **Timeline**
>
> **March 24, 1832**
> Treaty of Cusseta is signed by the Creeks surrendering the rest of their land east of the Mississippi river.
>
> **October 20, 1832**
> Treaty of Pontotoc was signed with the Chickasaw.
>
> **December 18, 1832**
> Benton County, Alabama is established, being named in honor of Thomas Hart Benton U.S. Senator of Missouri. It was later renamed as Calhoun County.
>
> **December 18, 1832**
> Randolph County, Alabama is established, being named in honor of John Randolph of Virginia, a member of the U.S. Senate.

Timeline

December 18, 1832
Talladega County, Alabama is established, being named in honor of the Creek Indian Town, Talladega.

December 18, 1832
Coosa County, Alabama is established, being named in honor of the Alabama Indian Tribe.

December 18, 1832
Tallapoosa County, Alabama is established, but the source of the Native American name is unclear.

December 18, 1832
Chambers County, Alabama is established, being named in honor of Henry Chambers, Senator from Alabama.

family a little gift of money. Everybody got apples and striped store candy.

Then the slaves went back to the quarters to enjoy Christmas in their own way. They decorated with cedar boughs and sang. They jigged and played games and probably had as good a time as the white folks at the big house. At ten o'clock that night, the foreman blew his horn and all the slaves had to go to bed. Much to their dismay, the next day work went on as usual.

Cotton Picking Time

Cotton-picking season was a big time. To make a good picker, one must start young. Hands who are put to picking after they are grown cannot keep up, because they have to hold the stalk with one hand and pick with the other. Good pickers pick with both hands at the same time, and the best pickers go between the rows picking both sides at once. Each morning, the pickers took their places with a tow sack to put the cotton in swung across their shoulders. When they had picked a sack full, they would empty it into a split basket and begin to pick again. At the end of the day, every worker's cotton would be weighed and carried to the cotton shed. Five hundred pounds was considered a good day's work, and the picker who could pick six hundred pounds always stood high with the overseer.

Every planter had his own gin. There were no steam gins. Eight mules were hitched to long beams that

Picking Cotton

moved the machinery. The gin cleaned the cotton and separated the lint from the seed. After this, the overseer would weigh the cotton, have it baled and marked ready to be carried to town.

Hog Killing Time

Every planter tried to raise all of his own meat. When a cold snap came in the fall, they would have a hog killing. The hams, shoulders, sides, and jowls were rubbed down with salt. Some of the meat was ground into sausage and packed down in lard. Then, all of it was hung on rafters in the smoke house, a slow fire of hickory wood was built on the earth floor, the door was closed, and the meat was left to smoke until it was cured.

There was a plentiful supply of backbones, spareribs, and other parts that had to be eaten at once or they would spoil. Much of the fat was cut into small pieces and put into pots with enough water to keep it from scorching. This was stirred constantly. When all the grease had been cooked out of the meat and the water had evaporated, the liquid was strained through cloth bags. The grease was now lard. The meat that was left was called cracklings. The cook at the big house kept some to make into cracklin' bread, and the rest was given to the slaves for the same purpose.

Crackling bread was made of meal, water, salt, and cracklings shaped into cakes and baked. My, how glad the slave's young children were when hog killing time came! It was almost, but not quite, as good as sorghum time. When sorghum time came, everybody could make as much sorghum candy as he could eat.

> **Timeline**
>
> **December 18, 1832**
> Russell County, Alabama is established, being named in honor of Colonel Gilbert C. Russell.
>
> **December 18, 1832**
> Macon County, Alabama is established, being named in honor of Nathaniel Macon, U.S. Senator from North Carolina.
>
> **December 18, 1832**
> Barbour County, Alabama is established, being named in honor of James Barbour, who served as Governor of Virginia.
>
> **December 18, 1832**
> Sumter County, Alabama is established, being named in honor of General Thomas Sumter of South Carolina.

Timeline

1833
Ross Landing becomes Chattanooga, Tennessee after the removal of the Cherokees.

1833
John Coffee dies in Florence, Alabama. Coffee played an important role in the founding of Florence.

1833
Daniel Pratt built a cotton gin factory in Autauga County.

November 12, 1833
Meteor shower: "The Night Stars Fell on Alabama".

Candle Making

Many things that are bought in stores today had to be made at home in those days. Candles were made on the plantation from beef tallow or fat. The fat was rendered like lard, and wicks were made of twisted cotton yarn and hung in the middle of the candle molds. Then the melted tallow was poured into the molds and allowed to cool. The master bought wax candles to use in the parlor to provide additional light to read and write; there was a glass shade around the candlestick to keep the candle from flickering.

Mutton or sheep tallow was made like beef tallow and was mixed with herbs and used to rub chests, throats, and noses when for those who had colds. It was good for chapped hands, also. Mutton tallow for the big house was mixed with camphor and molded in cups. In those days, people did not have Vaseline or any kind of cold cream.

Soap Making

Almost all of the soap was made on the plantation. All the leftover grease and pieces of fat were saved for soap grease. Only wood was used for fires, so there were plenty of wood ashes. Special care was taken to save the hickory ashes. The ashes were put into a large hopper with holes in the bottom, and then water was poured over them. After the drip became strong enough to float an egg, it was saved for lye. The grease and water was put into a pot and cooked until the fat melted. After the fat cooled, it was skimmed off and mixed with the lye to make soap. Every slave cabin had to be scoured with soap once a week. The table, pots, and skillets had to be kept clean.

The Slave Quarters

All of the slaves except the house servants lived at the quarters, and the overseer had charge of them. The best leader among the slaves helped the overseer and was called the foreman.

The overseer's home was a cottage near the quarters so that he could see how the slaves were living and how the work was going on. He had to keep a plantation book and write in it the name of every slave and what the duties were of the individual slave. If the slave was ill, this had to be written down. The number of stock also had to be written down. The overseer would decide what, when, and where to plant and had to see to it that plenty of food for the slaves and stock was grown along with enough for the master's family. When the cotton was ginned, he had to see that it was bailed and marked for shipment.

Timeline

1834
The Muscle Shoals Canal opens, making travel on the Tennessee River more manageable.

1835-1837
Clement Comer Clay is the governor of the state of Alabama.

1835
Alabama gold rush begins only to peak the next year.

The Quarters

The slave houses were one-room log cabins whitewashed inside and out every spring. They were built in two long rows facing one another across a wide-open space. There were typically a number of shade trees and a large well close by.

Timeline

1835
Dr. James Marion Sims "the father of Modern gynecology" established a medical practice near Montgomery, AL. He later founded a Woman's Hospital in New York.

December 29, 1835
Treaty of New Echota is signed with the Cherokee surrendering the last of their land in Alabama.

January 9, 1836
DeKalb County, Alabama is established, being named in honor of Major General Baron Johan DeKalb. DeKalb County was once part of the Cherokee Nation and home of the famous Sequoyah.

January 9, 1836
Cherokee County, Alabama is established, being named in honor of the Native American tribe that made their homes in this area prior to the Indian Removal.

The overseer's house was at one end of the rows of cabins; the tool house, blacksmith's shop, carpenter's shop, saddler's shop, and the spinning and weaving room were at the other end. There was a large cabin set aside for a nursery for the children to stay in while their mothers were at work; an older woman lovingly referred to as "granny," looked after these children.

While the field hands were in the fields, their meals were sent out to them. In the winter, a fire was built near the field for the workers to rest and warm themselves when necessary.

Some slaves had their own chickens and a vegetable garden. Some planters allowed their slaves to sell the produce, but others thought they should eat it themselves.

The master had some of the slaves to cut and bring wood to the cabins so that when the hands came in from work, they would have fuel for fires. A big backlog was kept burning or covered with ashes, so it was easy to start a good fire.

So, for a long time, fire was kept carefully at the big house, as well as at the quarters. If the fire went out, a shovelful of coals was borrowed from some other fire, and with the aid of chips (which were plentiful), a new fire was started. The field hands usually stopped work at sunset. Every hand was expected to work ten acres of cotton and six acres of corn.

There was always a fiddler on the plantation and every Saturday night the quarters were lively with dancing, singing, and patting of hands and feet. There was a church for the slaves, and they were required to attend every Sunday. Besides the black minister, sometimes there was a white minister to preach to them.

In summer, when the cotton crop was laid by, the slaves would have a revival service. During this revival, there would be a great deal of singing. Some of the cherished songs were: *Swing Low, Sweet Chariot, Stand on the Rock, I Couldn't Hear Nobody Praying,* and *When the Roll is Called Up Yonder, I'll Be There.* Then there would be a baptizing in the creek with a great deal of shouting and praying.

The Way the Slaves Dressed

Slaves did not buy clothes. Every year, the master gave all slaves a suit of clothes and a pair of shoes and the women and girls were given a dress and two bandanna handkerchiefs. The slaves made all the cloth for the clothes on the plantation. The women's dresses and the men's shirts were woven in blue and white or brown and white checks.

Underclothes were unbleached cotton. The men's overalls were of heavy blue or brown jeans. All stockings and socks were knitted by the women on the plantation. The spinners and weavers on the plantation supplied all of the cloth used on the plantation.

The master generally ordered a case of shoes of assorted sizes, to ensure everybody would have shoes that fit. Then the saddler, who mended the saddles, harness, and other leather goods, would patch the shoes until the time came for everybody to have new ones. Shoes were considered something 'extra-fine' in summertime, but the slaves were comfortable without them. They would usually save a pair to wear to church. In the southern part of the state, it was so warm that the slaves rarely wore shoes.

CHAPTER 9
YEARS LEADING UP TO THE WAR

Vocabulary:

Vice-President	Intelligent	Statesman
Patriotic	Traitor	Released
Blockade	Brevet	Adjutant
Canvass	Political	Tariff
Campaign	Oath of Office	Secede
Artillery	Infantry	Arsenal
Cavalry	Navy	Conquer
Statesman	Patriotic	Released
Capitol		

Research Suggestions:

1. On what date did Alabama secede from the Union? Did everyone support this decision? Add your research findings to your *Alabama Timeline Journal Notebook*.

2. What happened in Winston County, Alabama? Add your research findings to your *Alabama Timeline Journal Notebook*.

3. There was a 1st Alabama Union Calvary during the War Between the States. Research this Calvary unit. Add your research findings to your *Alabama Timeline Journal Notebook*.

4. Federal forces invaded Huntsville, Decatur, Florence and Tuscumbia. When did this happen? Why did they choose these towns? Who was the general leading the Federal Army when they invaded these towns? What happened to the people living in these towns? Add your research findings to your *Alabama Timeline Journal Notebook*.

5. What battles were fought near your hometown? Write a paper about the battle. Add this

information to your Alabama Timeline Journal.

6. Research the blockades and the blockade-runners. Add this information into your *Alabama Timeline Journal Notebook*.

7. Research your area to locate any Confederate monuments in your area.

8. Research railroads and other transportation for cotton crops.
Where was the first railroad in Alabama? What year did the railroad first come to Alabama? How did the railroad change things for people and businesses in Alabama? Add your research findings to your *Alabama Timeline Journal Notebook*.

People & Places to Research:

Sallie Knox Taylor
William Rufus King
John Milner
Charles Christopher Sheats
Arsenal at Mount Vernon, Alabama
Great Naval Works & Arsenal at Selma
Fort Blakeley
Juliet Opie Hopkins
Augusta Evans Wilson

Zachary Taylor
Salt Mines
Jefferson Davis
Arsenal
Amelia Gorgas
Octavia Le Vert
Mount Vernon
Winston County

Science & Nature Study:

Passion Flower
Ginkgo Tree
Alabama Chinkapin
Weeping Willow
Poison Sumac

Goldenrod
Dogwood
Pecan
Black Locust
Poison Ivy

Horse Mint
Sassafras
Black Willow
Poison Oak

Map Work:

Mark these towns on your map:
Birmingham
Dothan
Hoover

Montgomery
Decatur
Florence

Huntsville
Gadsden

Mark the battles that you locate on your map.

Mark the following towns on your map:
Huntsville   Decatur   Tuscumbia
Florence

Locate & Label Winston County, Alabama.

Dramatization Suggestions:

Write a drama about one of the many remarkable events that occurred in Alabama during the war. Put together a production and invite family and friends.

Local & Family History:

Go to your local library's genealogy room and look up information about your city/county and family. Call your grandparents and older family members to learn what you can about the family.

1. What was the name of the first school in your area? Who was it named after? Add all of this information to your *Alabama Timeline Journal Notebook*.

Events Leading Up to The Civil War

Before the war, most of the blacks in the South were slaves. They provided most of the hard labor needed on large plantations. There were many people that saw slavery as wrong. The people in the Northern states that saw slavery as wrong spoke out often. They began working to help slaves gain their freedom.

The people in the Southern states were not happy with this because they saw the slaves as their personal property, in much the same way that Northern factory owners saw their businesses as personal property. The Southerners seemed to think if the South didn't interfere with the Northern factories owners, the Northerners shouldn't interfere with the Southern plantation owners.

The North and the South disputed over this and many other issues such as tariffs for many years. The Southern states strongly believed in the 'states rights' to govern themselves. This simply means they believed that the state government had more control over what laws were made and how the state ran business than the federal government.

The United States had elected Abraham Lincoln as president. Many people called Abraham Lincoln "The Black Republican." The Confederate States elected Jefferson Davis, of Mississippi, president. Jefferson Davis was sworn in as the President of the Confederate States on February 18, 1861, on the front porch of the capitol in Montgomery.

The war officially began on April 12, 1861, when South Carolina fired on Fort Sumter. But the intensity leading up to the war began long before the first shots were fired. The

Timeline

January 9, 1836
Marshall County, Alabama is established, being named in honor of famous U.S. Chief Justice John Marshall.

1836
Texas wins independence from Mexico. Many of the men who fought in the Creek Indian War, also fought for Texas' independence from Mexico.

1836
Joseph Wheeler was born.

1837-1841
Martin van Buren is President of the United States.

1837-1841
Arthur P. Bagby is the governor of the state of Alabama.

1838
Maria Fearing was born a slave on a plantation in Gainesville, Alabama.

> **Timeline**
>
> **1840**
> Alabama Census
> Alabama Population: 590,756
> White Population: 335,185
> African-American: 255,571
> Slave Population: 253,532
> Free Black Population: 2,039
>
> **1841**
> William Henry Harrison is President of the United States.
>
> **1841-1845**
> John Tyler is President of the United States.
> Benjamin Fitzpatrick is the governor of the state of Alabama.
>
> **1841**
> Coffee County, Alabama is established, being named in honor General John Coffee.
>
> **1841**
> Julia Tutwiler is born in Tuscaloosa.
>
> **1845-1849**
> James K. Polk is President of the United States.

tension between northern and southern states had been heating up for many years. There were some events that occurred prior to the war that brought the country to the boiling point of war.

First, you must understand that the intensity between the northern and southern states was manifested in the U.S. government—between the Senators and Congressmen, who were the delegates from both areas. The disagreements between the states were discussed by these men and many times the debates would become heated to the point of physical violence. As you can imagine, this kind of tension made it very hard for the statesman to work together making decisions for the country. There was great disparity in their convictions and beliefs.

Tariffs were a major source of contention between the northern and southern states. The tariff was a high percentage that was charged on the goods being brought into the country on the ships that were returning from delivering cotton.

Many in the South believed the North had imposed the tariff to control the south, forcing the South to trade with expensive northern businesses, even though many European countries could provide a better product for a more affordable price. As you can imagine, this did not make people happy. If the ships returned from Europe to the South empty it would not be as economically feasible for the ships to transport the cotton. At the time, cotton was 90% of the United States exports. The ships returning were numerous.

There was also the matter of the Lincoln and Douglass debates leading up to the country dividing in war. Stephen A. Douglass had been a nationally known leader in the Democratic Party when the virtually unknown Abraham Lincoln challenged his seat as an Illinois Senator. Douglass was a popular democrat because of his work in securing the Kansas – Nebraska Act in 1854. Lincoln was well aware of the fact that he had to sell himself to the Illinois voters. To do this, he agreed to debate at seven different locations in the state, giving the people of Illinois the opportunity to come out and hear what each candidate had to offer the state.

Remember there were no televisions at that time. This is why they debated in many different locations, simply to ensure as many people as possible could hear them. Douglass was a popular state leader at this time, popular enough that the newspaper reporters began to follow the debates and report the details to newspapers which were published in other areas of the country.

There were a total of seven debates in 1858, from the top of Illinois to the bottom. At the end of the debates, Lincoln lost the senatorial race but had made a name as a Republican that would speak out against slavery. It was at this time that people begin to refer to Lincoln as the "Black Republican."

The debates from the Illinois senate race had fashioned Lincoln into a national figure that many believed would oppose slavery, standing against the institution of slavery from the office of president. When Lincoln lost the senate race, he was actually positioned for the Republican nomination for the presidency.

Timeline

1845-1847
Joshua L. Martin is the governor of the state of Alabama.

1846
The State Capital of Alabama is moved to Montgomery from Tuscaloosa.

1847-1849
Reuben Chapman is the governor of the state of Alabama.

December 29, 1847
Choctaw County, Alabama is established, being named for the Choctaw American Indian Tribe.

1849-1850
Zachary Taylor is President of the United States.

1849
Alabama State Capitol building is destroyed by fire.

1849-1853
Henry W. Collier is the governor of the state of Alabama.

> **Timeline**
>
> **1850-1853**
> Millard Fillmore is President of the United States.
>
> **1850**
> Alabama Census
> Alabama Population: 771,623
> White Population: 426,514
> African-American: 345,109
> Slave Population: 342,844
> Free Black Population: 2,265
> Cotton Production in Bales: 564,429
> Corn Production in bushels: 28,754,048
> Manufacturing Establishments: 1,026
>
> **February 12, 1850**
> Hancock County is established and named in honor of John Hancock, signer of the Declaration of Independence. Hancock county was later renamed Winston County.

Then on October 16, 1859, John Brown, along with the guerrilla troops he had put together, raided the arsenal at Harpers Ferry in West Virginia. He was planning to use the weapons in the arsenal to arm slaves to rise up against the whites across the Blue Ridge Mountain area. After thirty-six hours of fighting, with most of his men dead, John Brown was captured. He was found guilty of treason and hung by the neck until dead on December 2, 1859.

The interesting link between Lincoln and John Brown was they both were Republicans. Many people in the South believed John Brown would encourage slaves to rise up and kill their owners; some people in the South thought Abraham Lincoln could be just as dangerous.

Abraham Lincoln became the 16th President of the United States on March 4, 1861. There were four candidates that ran for the office of president that election year. The votes were split by the four, resulting in Lincoln winning the office of president. Lincoln had only won a few of the counties in the South, with only 39.95% of the votes. (At this time please refer to the website links available for further research of this election.)

The event at Harpers Ferry and Lincoln's election is what prompted the attack on Fort Sumter on April 12, 1861.

When Alabama made the decision to leave the United States, Winston County, Alabama decided that it would leave the state of Alabama and form the Free-State of Winston.

There were many people in the southern states that did not want to go to war. There were still strong feelings left from the American Revolution, building strong ties to the United States of America. Many people from North Alabama had loyalties to the Union that were much stronger than the loyalties to Alabama. This patriotism caused many divisions between families and friends.

> **Timeline**
>
> **1850**
> Fugitive Slave Law was established.
>
> **June 5, 1851**
> Uncle Tom's Cabin began distribution in chapter sections as a weekly serial in a magazine.
>
> **1851**
> Construction of Alabama's new capitol building was completed.

CHAPTER 10
WAR BETWEEN THE STATES

Vocabulary:

Recumbent	Knightly	Gentleman
Kearsarge	Yacht	Law of Nations
Surrender	Inspecting	Yankees
Rebels	Cavalry	Confederacy
Foundry	Plundering	Railhead
Union		

Research Suggestions:

1. Research Raphael Semmes and the sinking of "The Alabama." Add your research findings to your *Alabama Timeline Journal Notebook*.

2. Why was the Tennessee Valley such an active region for skirmishes during the Civil War? Add your research findings to your *Alabama Timeline Journal Notebook*.

3. What was Streight's Raid? What was he hoping to accomplish with his raids? Add your research findings to your *Alabama Timeline Journal Notebook*

4. Who was Nathan Bedford Forrest? What did he do to stop Streight's raiding? Add your research findings to your *Alabama Timeline Journal Notebook*.

5. Why were the communities of Tannehill, Brierfield, and Selma important? Why were some of the largest cavalry units in history assembled here? Add your research findings to your *Alabama Timeline Journal Notebook*.

6. Who were Wilson and Croxton? Where were some of the famous places they raided? Why did they choose these places? Add your research findings to your *Alabama Timeline Journal*

Notebook.

7. General Sherman was in Alabama during the war. Where was he in Alabama? Add your research findings to your *Alabama Timeline Journal Notebook*.

8. Why did Robert E. Lee surrender without discussing it with Jefferson Davis? Add your research findings to your *Alabama Timeline Journal Notebook*.

People & Places to Research:

Selma: The Arsenal of the South
Ulysses S. Grant
Admiral David Farragut
Fort Morgan
Abraham Lincoln
Alexander Stephens
Battle of Mobile Bay
Fort Gaines

Map Work:

Mark & label the following

Selma   Fort Morgan   Tannehill

Local & Family History:

Go to your local library's genealogy room and look up information about your city/county and family. Call your grandparents and older family members to learn what you can about the family.

1. Research the activities in your community or surrounding communities during the war. Were there battles in your area? Were there interesting people from your area that served in the confederate military? Did anyone in your family serve in the confederate military?

Timeline

1852
William Rufus King of Selma was elected Vice President of the United States. He died in his Selma, Alabama home, never actually serving as Vice President because of his health condition.

March 1852
Uncle Tom's Cabin is published into hardback selling 160,000 copies in the first 11 weeks.

1853-1857
Franklin Pierce is President of the United States.

1853-1857
John A. Winston is the governor of the state of Alabama.

1853
John Campbell of Mobile becomes Judge on the U.S. Supreme Court.

Becoming our Own Country

After the Southern states decided to become their own country, they knew each state had to have some kind of government. The states sent men from all over Alabama and the other Southern states to Montgomery, Alabama, to plan this new government. The Southern states decided to call themselves The Confederate States of America. There was wild rejoicing on February 18, 1861; bands played, flags waved, and speeches were made. The Southern people believed that they were to have a country all their own.

Although the capitol of the Confederate States was later moved to Richmond, Virginia; Alabama is proud that Montgomery was the first capitol. This historic city is still called "The Cradle of the Confederacy."

The United States had a large army and planned to conquer the Confederate States. One important part of this plan was to position ships at all the Confederate ports so that the South could not ship their cotton. Without the money from cotton crops, they could not pay for supplies. These blockades were also designed to keep them from bringing in necessary supplies.

Let us suppose that you were living in Alabama between 1861 and 1865. Your fathers, uncles, and older brothers, would most likely be in the Confederate Army. For the most part, the only people left at home were old men, women, children, and slaves. First one army and then the other would march through the country. If the soldiers were dressed in gray, you would be glad to see them. If, however, they were dressed in blue, you would feel frightened. All the silver and jewelry of the family would be hidden somewhere. Your mother would have taken a trusted old slave with her to bury it, but you would not know where.

You no longer had a variety of good things to eat. First, the soldiers had to be fed; the people at home had to eat what was left. Cornbread, hominy, and grits took the place of wheat bread. This would not make much difference for you, however, because southern children are fond of those foods. You would miss having sugar, though. Sorghum or molasses, which the slaves called "long sweet'nin," had taken the place of sugar, or "short sweet'nin."

Coffee came from South America, so when the blockade cut off the supply line, corn and sweet potatoes cut into cubes and parched had to be used as substitutes. Fortunately, lye from the ash hoppers and meat grease carefully saved would give a fair soap, but where were you to get salt?

The earthen floor of the smoke house was filled with salt from the drippings of the meat. This earth was dug up and put into a bucket. Then water was poured over it to soak out the salt. Then it was poured off and boiled until all of the water was gone. In the bottom of the vessel would be pure white salt.

What would you do when your clothes were worn out? The South raised cotton, but it was shipped to Northern mills to be made into cloth. There were only a few cotton mills in the South. However, there were still many spinning wheels and looms. These were used to make heavy cottonade. You would be glad indeed to get cottonade. Carpets were cut up for army blankets; old leather, carriage and buggy curtains were used to make shoes. Linen sheets were torn into strips to make bandages for the wounded. You would gather long dry grass and weave it to make straw hats. War times are indeed hard times.

> ### Timeline
>
> **1854**
> Lincoln & Douglass Debates.
>
> **1856**
> Alabama Coal Mining Company begins operations near Montevallo.
>
> **1856**
> East Alabama Male College is established at Auburn by the Methodist Church. Later it becomes Auburn University.
>
> **March 6, 1857**
> The United States Supreme Court made the decision with a 6-3 vote in the Dred Scott case, that a slave taken to a free state did not become free.
>
> **1857-1861**
> James Buchanan is President of the United States.

Timeline

1857-1861
Andrew B. Moore is the governor of the state of Alabama.

January 22, 1858
Winston, County Alabama formerly Hancock County was renamed to Winston in honor of Governor John A. Winston.

January 29, 1858
Calhoun County, Alabama is established, being named in honor of John C. Calhoun. The county was originally established on December 18, 1832 as Benton County, being named in honor of Thomas Hart Benton. Although Benton was a slave holder, he began to view slavery as wrong.

Music During the War

Throughout history, soldiers have loved to sing songs during wartime. The favorite song of the Union soldiers was *Yankee Doodle*, an old song of the Revolutionary War. The favorite song of the Confederates was *Dixie*, a rather new song at that time, composed by Dan Emmet, a member of a minstrel company. Some other favorite songs were *Wait for the Wagon, Goober Pease, Tramp, Tramp, Tramp, The Boys are Marching,* and *The Girl I Left Behind Me.*

After the children sing *Wait for the Wagon*, take time to discuss the meaning of the lyrics. Be sure to tell them that Alexander Stephens was the Vice President of the Confederate States.

States that Founded the Confederacy

Which states seceded and became part the Confederate States? There was Virginia, North Carolina, South Carolina, Georgia, Florida, Alabama, Mississippi, Louisiana, Texas, Arkansas, and Tennessee.

Sing the names of these states to the tune of *One Little, Two Little, Three Little Indians*.

Sing:
"Virginia, North and South Carolina,
Georgia, Florida, Alabama, Mississippi,
Louisiana, Texas, Arkansas, and Tennessee.
These are the Confederate States."

Although there are many officers in an army, there must be one officer who is over everybody else and plans what must be done. We call this officer the commander-in-chief. General Robert E. Lee became the commander-in-chief of the Confederate army, and General Ulysses S. Grant became the commander-in-chief of the United States army.

Soldiers must wear uniforms. The United States uniform was blue, and the Confederate uniform was gray, so you often hear the armies spoken of as the "Blue and the Gray."

The Confederates called the Union soldiers, "Yankees." The Union soldiers called the Confederate soldiers, "Rebels." This dreadful war lasted four years.

On the following pages are some of the songs which were sung by the soldiers of the Confederate Army and people of the South during the war. *The Girl I Left Behind Me* was probably written in 1758. For almost a hundred years, it has been the soldiers' and sailors' farewell song as they went forth to war. When the children sing *The Girl I Left Behind Me*,

Timeline

1858
After serving as a lieutenant in the Mexican war, Edmund Winston Pettus, moves to Cahaba, Alabama to practice law.

October 1858
Institute for the Deaf & Blind opens in Talladega.

1859
Medical College of Alabama is established in Mobile.

1859
The last slave ship coming to the United States, docked at Mobile.

1859
John Brown attacks the arsenal at Harpers Ferry, Va. planning to arm slaves for an uprising.

> **Timeline**
>
> **1860**
> Alabama Census
> Alabama Population: 964,201
> White Population: 526,271
> African-American: 437,770
> Slave Population: 435,080
> Free Black Population: 2,690
> Cotton Production in Bales: 989,955
> Corn Production in bushels: 33,226,282
> Manufacturing Establishments: 1,459
>
> **1860**
> Five northern states allow blacks to vote.
>
> **November 1860**
> Abraham Lincoln is elected president; he was not on the Alabama ballot.

those who whistle well, may whistle to imitate the high, clear notes of the fife.

The Girl I Left Behind Me

If ever I live to get over this war,
And the Yankee boys don't find me,
I'll wend my way back to North Alabama,
To the Girl I left behind me.

And since to war I went away,
Her letters oft remind me
That I promised never to gainsay
The girl I left behind me.

Tramp, Tramp, Tramp, the Boys are Marching was sung in both armies.

The Confederate chorus was:

Tramp, tramp, tramp, the boys are marching.
Cheer up, comrades, and be gay:
For beneath the Southern skies
We shall breathe the air again
Of our own beloved home so far away.

A Confederate Hospital

If you had been in Florence, Alabama, during the War Between the States, you would have been interested in an old brick house painted white on the northeast corner of Seminary Street and Jackson Highway.

On the long front porch, you would have seen men in gray uniforms sitting in rolling chairs with their legs bound in splints, men with one arm missing, men with heads bandaged, men on crutches. Through the windows might come the sounds of groans from men who have been badly wounded. This building served as a Confederate hospital.

Professional nurses such as we have today, did not exist; everyone in town helped nurse the soldiers. It was common to see the girls of the town bringing rolls of linen to the hospital for the wounded. There was no way to purchase bandaging, so Southern women improvised by tearing up sheets and tablecloths to use instead.

It might be that the girls were bringing something especially good to eat, like some chicken soup or some calves' foot jelly. Perhaps they had baked a war cake. Do you know how war cake was made?

It was hard to get flour, so the cook would sift cornmeal through a sifter and then through cheesecloth. This fine meal was war flour. There was no sugar, so sorghum, or "long sweet'nin," was used instead. A cake made out of war flour with "long sweetening" was called war cake and tasted good when it was the best you could get.

You must not think that life was all hardship and tears at the hospital. The men were brave. They loved to brag about their officers and the brave things they did. As soon as they felt well enough, they even laughed and joked with each other and with the nurses who were so kind and friendly. Some of the men had guitars, banjos, Jew's-Harps, or French harps. They enjoyed singing war songs.

> **Timeline**
>
> **December 20, 1860**
> South Carolina secedes from the Union.
>
> **1861-1863**
> John Gill Shorter is the governor of the state of Alabama.
>
> **1861-1865**
> Abraham Lincoln is President of the United States.
>
> **January 4, 1861**
> Alabama Militia seized federal forts Gaines, Mt. Vernon and Morgan.
>
> **January 7, 1861**
> Secession Convention.
>
> **January 11, 1861**
> Alabama secedes by a 61 to 39 vote.

The Alabama

The blockade gave the South a great deal of trouble. The Confederate States had no real navy, but they did have some ships that sailed the seas and attacked the United States. Merchantmen took their cargo, saved the people aboard, but burned the ships and did many other things that pirates do. Yet these ships were not pirate ships. They were considered privateers, because President Jefferson Davis gave them papers saying that they were

Timeline

February 4, 1861
The Confederate Conference meets in Montgomery. Jefferson Davis is elected President of the Confederacy.

March 4, 1861
Abraham Lincoln is sworn in as 16th president of the United States.

April 12, 1861
The Civil War begins when South Carolina fires on Fort Sumter.

May 1861
The capitol of the Confederate States is relocated from Montgomery to Richmond, Virginia.

The Alabama

Raphael Semmes

acting for the Confederate States, not for themselves.

The greatest privateer was *The Alabama*, but it never came near Alabama nor any other of the Confederate states. *The Alabama* was built in England and at first was known as *The 290*. The United States complained to England that she was allowing a ship to be built for the Southern States that were rebelling against the United States. The Queen of England said that this must not be done.

In spite of the Queen's order, when *The 290* was finished in August 1862, it was put out to sea on a trial trip—so it was said. When it reached the Azores Islands in the Atlantic Ocean, it was given over to Captain Raphael Semmes of the Confederate States. He christened the ship, *The Alabama*, named for his home state. Semmes lived in Mobile, Alabama.

Captain Semmes made *The Alabama* the terror of the seas. He sailed *to* and *fro*, *thither* and *yon*, and in two years he captured sixty-five Union merchantmen. Needless to say, the United States vessels were looking for him everywhere.

In June 1864, *The Alabama* sailed into port at Cherbourg, France. According to the law of nations, it could not stay there long. A United States ship, *The Kearsarge*, took its place outside the harbor and waited for *The Alabama* to come out. Captain Semmes knew there was to be a serious fight, but he expected to win. However, there was one important thing that Captain Semmes did not know. *The Kearsarge* had chains along her hull under the water line. This made her an ironclad ship.

The Alabama was so famous that many English and French ships were positioned to watch the fight. *The Alabama* fought bravely and well, but she had no chance against the ironclad *Kearsarge*. In a short while, *The Alabama* began to sink. Captain Semmes had the Confederate flag hauled down as a sign of surrender. The men jumped into the sea. *The Kearsarge*, for some reason, failed to send out boats to rescue them and unfortunately, some were drowned. Captain Semmes was picked up by the owner of an English yacht, *The Deer Hound*, and carried to London.

The English people treated Captain Semmes with great honor, for they loved a gallant fighter. His sword was at the bottom of the sea, so they gave him a handsome new one. An English lady made him a beautiful silk flag that is now in a glass case at the capitol at Montgomery.

The United States wanted England to give up Captain Semmes as a prisoner of war. England, however, said no because Captain Semmes had not been captured. Later, Captain Semmes ran the blockade and entered the Confederate States. He was named admiral of the Confederate Navy. The trouble was that there were so few ships, and they were so small, that they really did not make a navy.

> **Timeline**
>
> **January 22, 1862**
> The future Dr. Luther Hill is born in Montgomery; he was elected 5 terms as U.S. Senator representing Alabama.
>
> **February 1862**
> Southern troops defended the Tennessee Valley until federal occupations.
>
> **April 1862**
> Federal troops enter Huntsville.
>
> **June 1862**
> The C.S.S. Alabama sank off the coast of France.
>
> **January 1863**
> Abraham Lincoln signs and enacts the Emancipation Proclamation.

After the war was ended, Admiral Semmes was in prison for a while. The United States threatened to hang him as a pirate, but we know he was not a pirate. When he was released from prison, he returned to Mobile and was greatly respected. You may want to read his book, *Service Afloat*, which tells of the daring deeds of the captain of *The Alabama* and his brave crew.

Brave Emma Sansom

In the city of Gadsden, there is a monument to a young girl who did a very brave thing.

Alabama had one furnace which made iron for the guns and cannon balls used by the Southern soldiers. General Rosecrans, a general of the North, decided to destroy this furnace.

General Rosecrans sent a brave soldier, General Streight, into Alabama with a large number of men. They were to take away or destroy everything they thought would be of help to the South. These soldiers rode on horseback. General Forrest, a Southern soldier and a very brave man, found out what General Streight was trying to do. He did not have as many soldiers as General Streight, but his men were brave and willing to do anything to help the South. General Forrest made up his mind to drive General Streight's army out of Alabama before it could destroy the furnace. His men rode eagerly away with him to help carry out this vital mission.

General Streight and his men came down into Alabama, taking cannons and whatever else they desired as they went along. Then they hurried on to keep the Southern soldiers from catching them.

Timeline

April 1863
A.D. Streight surrenders to Nathan B. Forrest in Cherokee County.

1863
Sister Chrysostom Moynahan is born. She would become a pioneer in Alabama's health care.

1864
George Washington Carver is born in a one room log cabin in Missouri as a slave.

July 1864
General Rousseau destroys part of Montgomery.

August 5, 1864
David Farragut wins the Battle of Mobile Bay, giving the Union forces control of the bay.

General Forrest and his men rode fast to catch them. They hardly stopped to rest. When they came to the Warrior River, they were so tired that they had to stop. Their poor horses were worn out. Some of the men kept watch, while the others rested or fed the horses. Soldiers call this doing guard duty.

Everything was very still when suddenly one of the guards called, "Halt! Who goes there?" The soldiers sprang to their feet and seized their guns. Then everybody stared and smiled. There stood three girls. Each girl had a bridle over her arm, with a horse following. Each girl held a gun, and in front of each walked a soldier from the Northern army. These three girls had caught the three soldiers and were bringing them as prisoners to General Forrest. General Forrest thanked the brave girls and gave them the horses of the Northern soldiers.

By this time, General Streight was riding as fast as he could to escape from General Forrest. When he and his men came near Gadsden, they crossed Black Creek by a bridge. The water was high in the creek. "Ah," said the Northern general, "if we burn this bridge, the Confederate soldiers cannot get across." So the Northern soldiers broke up a wooden fence for fuel and set the bridge on fire.

> **Timeline**
>
> **August 23, 1864**
> Fort Morgan is defeated.
>
> **January 31, 1865**
> The Thirteenth Amendment to the Constitution of the United States is proposed.
>
> **April 5, 1865**
> Abraham Lincoln dies after being shot at Ford Theater.
>
> **1865-1869**
> Andrew Johnson is President of the United States.
>
> **1863-1865**
> Thomas H. Watts is the governor of the state of Alabama.
>
> **1865-1865**
> Lewis E. Parsons is the governor of the state of Alabama, appointed by Union occupation.

General Forrest was coming so fast that he was close behind the Northern soldiers. Near the creek he met a lady, Mrs. Sansom, and her two daughters. They showed him the burning bridge and the Northern soldiers guarding it. When General Forrest and his men tried to cross it, shots came thick and fast from the other side. If the Southern soldiers could not cross the creek, Streight's men would escape.

"Is there no other bridge?" General Forrest asked the ladies.

> **Timeline**
>
> **1865**
> April Croxton burns the University of Alabama.
>
> **1865**
> Wilson's troops raid Alabama destroying the Selma arsenal.
>
> **1865-1867**
> Robert M. Patton is the governor of Alabama.
>
> **1865**
> Freedmen's Bureau is formed to help freed slaves.
>
> **1865**
> U.S. Congress refuses to accept Alabama's new Constitution.

They said there was not. Then one of the girls, whose name was Emma, pushed her sunbonnet back from her face and stepped up to the general. "I know where there is a ford," she said, "a blind ford, my father called it. It is down in our pasture. Our cows used to cross there sometimes." By a ford, Emma meant a place in the creek where the water was not too deep for cattle to wade through. "Who can show me this ford?" the general asked quickly. "I can," Emma answered. There was not a minute to lose. The general pulled his horse close to a mound of dirt by the side of the road. Emma had already climbed to the top of it. The general reached down to help her, but Emma sprang on the horse behind him before he could touch her. Mrs. Sansom and Emma's sister were crying, "Come back, Emma, you will be killed!" But Emma knew that she must help General Forrest. Bullets from the other side of the creek were flying about them as they rode off, but Emma clung tightly to General Forrest and told him the way to go.

Soon the general and the girl came to the edge of the woods. There were no trees to hide them from the enemy now. Then Emma showed how brave she was. We have her story in a letter she wrote to a friend after she was grown.

"When we got close to the creek, I said, 'General Forrest, I think we had better get down off the horse, as we are now where we might be seen.' We both got down and crept through the bushes. When we were right at the ford I happened to be in front, and the Yankees began firing. General Forrest stepped quickly between me and the Yankees, saying, 'I am glad to have you for a pilot, but I am not going to make breastworks of you.'"

Whizz! A bullet went right through Emma's gingham skirt. It frightened the general when he saw the danger the girl was in. But she laughed. "They only hurt my skirt!" she said. The soldiers on the other side did not wish to harm such a brave girl! They stopped firing.

Emma took her sunbonnet off and waved at them with a smile. The Northern soldiers smiled back and cheered!

Emma showed General Forrest where to ford the creek and told him where to come out on the other side. When he took his men over, he followed her directions. They crossed the creek without trouble and began to ride after the Northern soldiers harder than ever.

When the Confederates at last caught the Northern soldiers, they took General Streight and nearly all of his men as prisoners. What made the Northern soldiers stop firing and smile at brave Emma Sansom as she showed General Forrest the way? Do you smile when you are in trouble or feeling badly? How much is a cheerful smile worth?

When you go to the capitol in Montgomery, be sure to look at the picture of brave Emma Sansom and remember how she helped the Southern soldiers.

The Surrender

Although the Confederates fought bravely and General Lee was a great general, there came a time when they could fight no longer. There were twenty-one Northern states and only eleven Southern states. There were more people, more money, and more factories creating more supplies in the North than in the South. So at last the South had to give up. General Lee surrendered to General Grant in Appomattox, Virginia on April 9, 1865.

General Grant, in his memoirs, tells the story of the surrender very simply without any boasting. He describes himself as dressed in an old blue uniform in which he had been inspecting his troops. He describes General Lee as very handsome, dressed in a new suit of Confederate gray, with the sword presented to him by the State of Virginia at his side. He looked like a victorious general.

The two generals saluted, talked a few minutes, and then planned for the surrender of the Confederate army. When General Grant learned that most of the Confederate soldiers were riding their own horses, not those of the Confederate Government, he said that they could take their horses home, as they would be needed for spring plowing. The country had to begin to rebuild at this point and the horses would be greatly needed for the next spring planting season.

CHAPTER 11
RECONSTRUCTION

Vocabulary:

Curfew   Lanterns   Chemist
Surname

Research Suggestions:

1. If Lincoln had lived to see the South through reconstruction, do you think he would have made things easier for the South? If so, how?

2. What was the Wade/Davis Bill? When was Alabama readmitted to the Union?

3. Who was the first Republican elected as governor after Alabama was readmitted to the Union?

4. Northern men came into the South and did things that made it very hard on the Southern soldiers. Raising taxes was one of the many things they did. How did this affect the area you live in? What did people do to pay these taxes?

5. What did Jefferson Davis do after the war? What happened to his children?

6. Why did John Wilkes Booth murder Abe Lincoln?

People & Places to Research:

Samuel Minturn Peck
Henry A. Loveless
Cudjo Lewis
Shandy Wesley Jones

William Henry Holtzclaw
James Thomas Rapier
Martha Foster Crawford
Theodore Hill

Burton H. Hudson
Lloyd Leftwich
Horace King

Science & Nature Study:

Bald Eagle	Cooper's Hawk	Northern Bobwhite
Eastern Screech Owl	Redheaded Woodpecker	Barn Swallow
Sweetgum	Eastern Cottonwood	Sycamore
Virginia Pine	Eastern White Pine	Poplar (Tulip tree)
Yellow Flicker		

Project Suggestions:

1. Make posters of various methods of lighting, beginning with the torch.

2. Discuss the various uses of cotton, cottonseed, and cotton stalks. Make a poster about cotton.

Map Work:

Add the following locations on the map:
Birmingham

Local & Family History:

Go to your local library's genealogy room and look up information about your city/county and family. Call your grandparents and older family members to learn what you can about the family.

1. Go to the genealogy department at your library. Ask the librarian to help you look up old newspaper articles. If you explain you are trying to learn local history, he or she will be most helpful. Most of the librarians in the genealogy departments are very pleased if someone is trying to learn local history. We have found the genealogy department to be the most helpful department in the library.

Reconstruction

Reconstruction was a particularly important part of the Northern war plan. The North claimed to be fighting the war to restore the Union. There was a great debate over the issue of Reconstruction. Abraham Lincoln's plan stated that as soon as he had appointed a governor and 10% of the states voters had signed oaths of loyalty to the Union that the state would no longer be considered in rebellion and that they could send representatives to Washington D.C. Arkansas, Louisiana, and Tennessee all complied with Lincoln's requirements, but Congress would not accept them back in the Union.

Instead, they passed the Wade/Davis Bill, which required fifty percent of the state's voters to sign oaths of loyalty to the Union before the state could be accepted back into the Union. Lincoln never signed the Wade/Davis Bill into law.

In April of 1865, Lincoln was assassinated and Andrew Johnson became president. Johnson adopted the Wade/Davis Bill with some slight modifications. He offered all Confederate soldiers full amnesty if they would sign an oath of loyalty to the Union, declare the cession null and void, agree to pay off the debt incurred by the Union during the war, adopting the 13th amendment and declare slavery illegal in the state constitutions. As soon as 50% of a state's voters had complied and the said requirements were fulfilled, the state was allowed to rejoin the Union.

Alabama was re-admitted to the Union in February of 1868. Reconstruction with the occupation of federal

Timeline

1866
The Ku Klux Klan is founded in Pulaski, Tennessee by Nathan Bedford Forrest.

February 15, 1866
Elmore County, Alabama is established, being named in honor of General John A. Elmore.

July 24, 1866
Tennessee was readmitted to the Union.

November 30, 1866
Crenshaw County, Alabama is established, being named in honor of Judge Anderson Crenshaw.

December 6, 1866
Lee County, Alabama is established, being named in honor of General Robert E. Lee.

December 6, 1866
Cleburne County, Alabama is established, being named in honor of Major General Patrick Cleburne.

troops lasted for 12 years, from 1865-1877, but the effects of the war have lasted much longer.

The Slaves Freed

We covered much about how the slaves lived on the old plantation. Once the war ended, things were much different for the freed slaves. One day, soon after General Lee surrendered to General Grant, the master of the plantation had someone ring the plantation bell, and of course, all the slaves came at once to the big house. They knew what the white folks were doing because of what was called the "grapevine telegraph." That is, if a slave heard white men talking, he would repeat what he had heard to the next slave he met, and they would carry the news to others they met. In this way, word flew quickly from mouth to mouth until all the slaves knew the latest news. So even before they were told by the master, the slaves knew that freedom had come, and had begun to sing songs in gratitude and celebration of freedom.

At first, there was wild rejoicing among them, but when they returned to their cabins, their feelings changed. Where were they to go? What were they to do? The old men and women were frightened. "Ole mars'er" was the only person they could rely on, and the old cabin was the only home they had ever known. The younger ones were anxious to see the world. They felt that they were not free if they had to stay on the plantation and work. Many of them left for a short while and then came back home to the plantation. Others wandered away to try their freedom and see how it felt to be free, and to vote, and to hold office. Of course, they had to work to live, and they

Timeline

December 6, 1866
Clay County, Alabama is established, being named in honor of the U.S. senator of Kentucky Henry Clay.

January 30, 1867
Hale County, Alabama is established, being named in honor of Confederate Colonel Stephen F. Hale.

February 4, 1867
Jones County, Alabama is established, later to be renamed Lamar County.

February 6, 1867
Colbert County, Alabama is established, being named in honor of Chickasaw Chiefs George and Levi Colbert.

October 1867
The new government for the state of Alabama begins to form with Northern leaders setting it up.

1867-1868
Wager Swayne is appointed as a military governor of Alabama during reconstruction.

did know how to work hard. But there was a problem; around 500,000 slaves were freed in Alabama alone and there was no money.

The war had just bankrupted Alabama along with all the other southern states. There was lots of work but no money to pay anyone. People were starving to death because of the lack of food. There was also a crippling lack of medical care. Many of the slaves that had been set free got into trouble trying to get the things needed to take care of themselves. Others worked as servants or at their trades and became good citizens. Some moved out west and to other places. But many went back to the plantations that had always been home. This is when the development of sharecropping began to be established.

One thing that was needed for the blacks as freedmen was a surname. Up to this point, they only had one name, such as Jim. If there were several men named Jim in one place, one might be Black Jim and another Yaller Jim, or he might be called by his mother's name, like Rhody's Jim.

While many blacks kept their masters' name, many felt that they would not really be free unless they chose a different one. Generally, they were known by their masters' name, so there are many blacks and white people with the same name in any old Southern town.

> **Timeline**
>
> **July 13, 1868**
> Alabama is readmitted to the Union with the Legislation's ratification of the State Constitution's 14th amendment.
>
> **1868**
> Etowah County, Alabama is established, being named for a Cherokee language term meaning "edible tree."
>
> **December 10, 1868**
> Escambia County, Alabama is established, being named in honor of the Native American word for river.
>
> **December 26, 1868**
> Geneva County, Alabama is established, being named after Geneva, New York.

Freedmen Bureau

Freedmen's Bureau as many called it or The Bureau of Refugees, also known as, Freedmen and Abandoned Lands was established in March 3, 1865 to address all matters concerning homeless freedmen within the states that were under reconstruction. The Bureau was not given a budget of its own, but was instead commissioned as a part of the War Department and depended upon the War Department for funds and staffing.

The main goal was providing emergency food, housing and medical care to all the people left with no way to care for themselves after they had been set free. By late 1865, the agency focused its work on helping the Freedmen adjust to their new lives. They arranged job opportunities and helped negotiate fair wages. Soon, the Bureau began to act as a military court that handled legal issues.

Freedman's Bureau & Abandon Lands

When the war was being fought, most males that were in good enough health to join, were away serving in the war. Most farms and plantations were operated by the women of the family. The plantation owners had slaves that greatly helped the women continue to operate the plantations. But the smaller farmers typically did not have slaves to help the wife, sister, or mother with the operation of the farm. As the Union Army pushed farther into the South, women did not feel safe with their husbands far away. Many women closed up their home, escaping to safety with family in other areas.

In many cases, these lands were not abandoned; the family was planning to return as soon as it was safe. Many families returned to find the government had placed other people on their land.

What was just as distressing about this situation is that the people placed on these properties had hope of a new life. But in many cases, the property was given back to the rightful owners.

Timeline

December 30, 1868
Baker County, Alabama is established, being named in honor of Alfred Baker. The name was changed in 1874 to Chilton County, Alabama.

1868-1870
William Hugh Smith is the governor of Alabama.

1869-1877
Ulysses S. Grant is President of the United States.

1869
Marie Bankhead Owen is born.

1869
Nathan Bedford Forrest, unhappy with the violence within the Ku Klux Klan, does everything in his power to disband the organization.

August 17, 1870
Richmond Pearson Hobson is born in Greensboro, Alabama.

> **Timeline**
>
> **1870-1872**
> Robert B. Lindsay, Alabama's only foreign born governor, is elected governor.
>
> **1870**
> Legislature accepts the 15th Amendment. This Amendment gives black men the right to vote.
>
> **1871**
> Maria Fearing begins school at the age of 33 at Talladega College.
>
> **1872**
> Under the Amnesty Act, former Confederate soldiers once again have the right to vote.
>
> **1872**
> Most federal troops leave Alabama.

Needless to say, with an enormous lack of funding and the incredible confusion over these properties, the Freedman's Bureau did not last beyond 1872.

But while the organization was in operation, it helped establish hundreds of schools for blacks.

The Freedman's Bureau, registered every freed man or woman willing to register with the organization, recording vast personal information. The bureau made huge promises of matching family members up that were lost from one another. They also promised monetary resources that were never delivered.

But the information collected, with all the detailed personal information, can now be accessed online. When researching family history, this information could be incredibly helpful to us today. Although the Bureau provided little help for the people that greatly needed them during Reconstruction, the information that they collected can be a fantastic research portal for us today.

CHAPTER 12
FREE MEN

Vocabulary:

Rapid
Laboratory
Amino acids

Errand
Lysine
Pentoses

Blizzard
Erosion

Research Suggestions:

1. Research Annie Rowen Forney Daugette. Add your research to your *Alabama Timeline Journal Notebook*.

2. Who was Booker T. Washington? What did he do to help George Washington Carver?

3. When was Tuskegee Institute founded? What were the academic goals of the institution?

4. What were some of the things that George Washington Carver suggested to the farmers? How did these suggestions affect their crops?

5. How many things did George Washington Carver create with peanuts? List your favorite peanut products in your *Alabama Timeline Journal Notebook*.

6. Research boll weevils. Add this information to your *Alabama Timeline Journal Notebook*.

7. What did some of the freed slaves do once they were free? Write a short essay and add it into your *Alabama Student Timeline Journal Notebook*.

8. Who was the first black elected to State Legislature? What year was the election?

People & Places to Research:

Richmond P. Hobson　　　Tuskegee Institute　　　Annie Lola Price
James Reese Europe　　　Agnes Ellen Harris　　　Thomas Edison
Booker T. Washington　　　Margaret Washington

Science & Nature Study:

Peanuts

Project Suggestions:

1. Draw or paste our state seal in your *Alabama Timeline Journal Notebook*.
2. Make homemade peanut butter using raw peanuts.

Map Work:

Mark the following town or city on your map:
Tuskegee　　　　　　　　Gainesville

Educating Blacks in Alabama

Few blacks could read or write when they became free. What to do about this was a serious question. There was little money in Alabama for white schools. As you can imagine, no attempt was made to educate the blacks.

Black education began earnestly in 1881. At this time, some Alabama gentlemen thought that the state should have a normal school for blacks, in order that black teachers might be trained to teach their people. They wrote to General Armstrong, President of Hampton Institute (a black school in Virginia), inquiring about a teacher. General Armstrong said that he did not know of any white man to suggest, but that he thought Booker T. Washington, a black man, could do the work.

Booker T. Washington, was born a slave on a Virginia plantation. After the war, he worked very hard to get an education. When he went to Hampton, he knew so little that the principal feared he could not enter the school. She told him to clean a certain room while she was trying to decide. He swept that room three times and dusted it four. When he had finished, it was spotless. The principal decided that he was a dedicated, earnest boy and should be given a chance. Booker continued to prove himself as a diligent student and patient teacher.

> **Timeline**
>
> **1872-1874**
> David P. Lewis is the governor of the state of Alabama.
>
> **Nov. 16, 1873**
> William Christopher Handy is born in a little log cabin in Florence, Alabama.
>
> **1874-1878**
> George S. Houston is the governor of the state of Alabama.
>
> **1874**
> Maud McKnight Lindsay is born.
>
> **1874**
> Chilton County, Alabama is established as Baker County and later renamed to Chilton in honor of William Parish Chilton, Sr. who was Chief Justice of the Alabama Supreme Court.

The Alabama Black School was established in Tuskegee, a small town in the Black Belt, where the blacks outnumbered the whites three to one. The state gave the school $2,000 a year to pay the teachers, but it gave no land and no building. The best place Booker T. Washington could get was an old shanty next to a Methodist Church. Soon some land was given to the school, and Booker T. Washington put his pupils to work making brick to build a house and making furniture for the school to use. Pupils and teachers worked together planting a garden and caring for chickens, pigs, and cows. This work served not only to supply food, but also to learn how to become good farmers.

Tuskegee Institute taught the Freed Blacks many other things in addition to reading and writing. Grooming was just as much a part of the daily education as a lesson in arithmetic. The pupils were taught to work, to save money, and to present themselves respectably.

Many Northern people were interested in Tuskegee Institute, and contributed money to the school. Now, the Tuskegee Institute owns much land and has many handsome buildings. These things, however, are not what make it a good school. Tuskegee is a good school, because it is training the blacks of Alabama to become intelligent, useful, and respected men and women.

George Washington Carver: The Strange Story of an Ex-Slave

At Tuskegee, there was an old black man named, George Washington Carver. The story of his life is like a fairy tale. He was born a slave, stolen by nightriders, and bought back by his master for an old racehorse. He became a wonderful chemist and artist. He had a hard time getting an education, but George took any job that came along and finally finished college. He received a doctor's degree in chemistry because of his remarkable work.

Booker T. Washington invited Dr. Carver to come to Tuskegee in 1896. He spent the rest of his career there. Although Thomas A. Edison tried to get him to work in his laboratory and he had many other positions offered to him, he stayed in Tuskegee.

He studied almost everything that grows along with the best soil for growing the different kinds of plants. George Washington Carver became such a good farmer that he soon

Timeline

August 1875
The people of Alabama elect 100 delegates to write a new Constitution.

1876
John Tyler Morgan is elected to the United States Senate where he served the state of Alabama for 30 years until his death.

1877
Lamar County, Alabama is established, being renamed from Jones County, Alabama to the current Lamar County, Alabama in honor of Lucius Quintus Cincinnatus Lamar, U.S. Senator from Mississippi.

raised a five hundred pound bale of cotton on an acre of land too poor to cultivate. Just think how important this was to the Alabama farmers.

He discovered new uses for many plants—especially peanuts, sweet potatoes, and cotton. From peanuts, he made milk, butter, cheese, coffee, pickles, dyes, and soap. All these combined totaled two-hundred and eighty-five different products! From the sweet potato, he made one-hundred and eighteen useful products, including: shoe blacking, ginger, ink, and dyes. The greatest discovery that he made from his study of cotton was how to produce a material that may be used in making roadbeds. This new use for cotton was thought to make the Alabama farmer rich.

George Washington Carver was an artist, as well as a farmer and chemist; he painted beautiful pictures. "I get my dyes," the old man told a visitor, "from Alabama clays. You remember what the Bible says, 'Look to the hills from whence cometh your help.' I did it. I looked to these Alabama hills, and I made these dyes from the clays I found there." Upon being asked if he was worried his paints would fade, he replied, "No sir; they won't fade. They've been in these Alabama hills a mighty long time without fading. They won't fade merely because I have taken them out and painted roses with them. Why should they fade?"

Dr. Carver did not sell his discoveries, but rather gave them to the world. Alabamians should feel grateful to this unselfish man for taking the simple, everyday things around him and using them to make life easier and happier for everyone.

> **Timeline**
>
> **1877-1881**
> Rutherford B. Hayes is President of the United States.
>
> **1878-1882**
> Rufus W. Cobb is the governor of the state of Alabama.
>
> **1879**
> Loraine Bedsole Tunstall is born. Tunstall would be the first woman to be appointed to an Alabama department head.
>
> **1880**
> Helen Keller is born in Tuscumbia, Alabama.
>
> **1881**
> James A. Garfield is President of the United States.

Timeline

1881
Joseph Wheeler serves several terms as U.S. Congressman from Alabama.

1881-1885
Chester A. Arthur is President of the United States.

July 4, 1881
Tuskegee Normal & Industrial Institute opens.

1881
Thomas Wesley Martin is born in Scottsboro, Alabama. He later became president of Alabama Power Company.

1881
Booker T. Washington becomes the president of Tuskegee Institute.

The Story of Maria Fearing

Maria Fearing was born on a plantation near Gainesville, Alabama in 1838. Her mother and father were slaves belonging to Mr. William Overton Winston, owner of the plantation.

Since Maria's mother and sister were household servants, Maria was allowed to go with them to work at the "big house." The real name for this plantation home was "Oak Hill," but the slaves called it the "big house."

Maria's first job was to play with the Winston children and take care of them. Her mistress, Mrs. Amanda Winston, was a very devout Christian. She spent much time teaching her children to be good Presbyterians. In the late afternoons, as little Maria Fearing sat rocking the smallest Winston child, she listened to the Bible stories that her mistress told. Mrs. Winston also told stories about the naked, barefoot children in Africa, who knew nothing about the true God. The stories about Africa made little Maria feel very sad, and she said, "I will go to Africa someday, if I can." And she did—but it was almost fifty years before her dream came true.

As Maria, grew up, her duties at the "big house" increased until she became a household servant, one of the best positions a slave could have on the plantation.

Maria Fearing remained with the Winston family until after the end of the War Between the States. Then, when all the slaves were freed, she moved to Gainesville and found a job as a household servant.

As time went by, Maria Fearing decided that she must learn to read so that she might study the Bible by herself. She found someone to teach her the alphabet, and with the aid of a copybook, she tried to teach herself to write. This way of learning was so slow that Maria became discouraged. Then, in 1871, she heard about a school called Talladega College for Blacks. In this school, a person could start at any age, and those who had no money could work to pay for their school fees and meals. Maria talked with her employer, and he encouraged her to go to school.

When she was thirty-three, Maria Fearing started school in the beginner's group at Talladega College. All of the members of her class were small children, and at first they laughed and made fun of her because she could not read or write. When she let the children know how much she loved them, she soon won their friendship and respect, and they forgot she was a grown woman. Maria learned so quickly that she was promoted from grade to grade until, within a few years, she had completed ninth grade. Now she was ready to teach others.

Maria Fearing taught in a two-room rural school near Anniston, Alabama for several years. Then she was asked to return to Talladega College, to become assistant matron of the boarding department.

> **Timeline**
>
> **1882**
> George Washington Carver is head of the agricultural department at Tuskegee.
>
> **1882-1886**
> Edward A. O'Neal is the governor of the state of Alabama.
>
> **1883**
> Dixie Bibb Graves is born. She is Alabama's first and only woman senator.
>
> **1885-1889**
> Grover Cleveland is President of the United States, 1st term.

In 1894, Doctor W. H. Shepard, a pioneer Presbyterian missionary to Africa, came to speak at Talladega College. He told of his work among the natives of Africa and asked for volunteers to assist him in his work. Maria Fearing was one of his most fascinated listeners. She remembered the story of the little, naked, barefoot children in Africa, which she had first heard about from her former mistress, and she realized that the time had come for her to go to Africa.

Maria was a true hero. She educated herself simply because she had such a strong desire to help others.

Controlling a group of people is no easy task. However, the most direct path to ruling over people against their will is dis-empowering them via the lack of education. This method has been used throughout history to gain power and control of people who were forced into slavery.

CHAPTER 13
THE SPANISH-AMERICAN WAR

Vocabulary:

Stegomyia	Anopheles	London
National Cemetery

Research Suggestions:

Research volunteers from Alabama for the Spanish-American War. Did anyone from your area fight in this war?

People & Places to Research:

William Crawford Gorgas	President William McKinley	Fighting Joe Wheeler

Science & Nature Study:

Sugar cane	Alfalfa crops in Alabama

Locate and research the largest pecan orchard in Alabama

Map Work:

1. Look at a United States Atlas. Locate Cuba. What is the distance from Florida to Cuba in miles?

2. Find and mark Havana.

The Spanish-American War

After living at peace for many years, in 1898, the United States had a war with Spain. Cuba was a colony of Spain, just as the United States used to a colony of England. Cuba wanted to be free and began to fight for her freedom.

We sympathized with Cuba. A number of U.S. citizens had sugar plantations in Cuba, so we sent a battleship called *The Maine* to Havana to see how U.S. citizens were being treated in Cuba. Unbelievably, *The Maine* was suddenly blown up and two hundred fifty-eight officers and men were killed.

The people of the United States believed Spain was to blame for this and they wanted to fight. A short time after the sinking of *The Maine*, the United States declared war on Spain. We said that we went to war because we were sorry for Cuba and wished to set her free. Our battle cry was "Remember *The Maine*!" The war was over in three months, and Cuba was set free.

General Grant once said that he hoped to see a son of General Lee fight in the same army with his son. It really happened that a Lee and a Grant both fought in this war. General Joseph Wheeler of Alabama, "Fighting Joe" of the War Between the States, was made a general in the United States Army and was nicknamed "Little Ex-Confed." "Rebels" who had once worn the gray fought side by side with "Yankees" who had worn the blue.

Fighting Joe Wheeler

Near Decatur, Alabama, is the beautiful home of brave General Joseph Wheeler. He is a hero and veteran of two wars. He was named "Fighting Joe" Wheeler because he would fight with all his might! It's hard to believe that a man who was known to be such a tender and gentle man could also be such a fighter. Here is part of a letter written by his daughter, Miss Annie Wheeler, in January of 1924.

"Never did a member of his family hear him say a harsh or angry word. Often he said, 'Never criticize anyone unless you have faced the same conditions and have done better; then don't!'"

Some of his friends tried to make him break this rule one day as he sat talking with them. They said unkind things about people they knew. Joe Wheeler did not join them. One man thought he might make the general break his rule by asking this question, "General Wheeler, what do you think of Satan?"

The general could hardly say any good of him. But he quietly answered, "I'll say this for him, he is mighty energetic." However, the general spoke the truth, even if he did speak gently, to him, truth was sacred.

Joseph Wheeler was gentle and kind as a boy. Yet when still a small boy he made up his mind to be a soldier. He planned for this and when he was old enough, he went to a school where soldiers are trained. This was the West Point Military Academy. It belongs to the people of the United States. Boys who do good work in school may go there to be trained as officers in the United States Army. When Joseph Wheeler finished his training at West Point, he was made lieutenant in the cavalry and sent to the West.

Afterward, he fought in the same war in which Emma Sansom helped General Forrest, the War Between the States. When the quarrel between the North and South began, Joseph Wheeler went to Tennessee, where he became a colonel in the army of the South. He planned quickly. When he made up his mind to do something, he did it with all his might. He was very successful and had great determination. Taking part in many battles, he was wounded three times, and had sixteen horses killed while he was on them!

He proved what a brave and wise man he was once when he cut off the Northern army from its supplies. The troops of General Rosecrans had their camp in Tennessee. Their supplies of guns, cannon balls, food, wagons were in Bridgeport, a town in northern Alabama.

There were two ways to go from the camp in Tennessee to the place of supply in Alabama. One road ran through the Sequatchie (See-kwat-chee) Valley, the other along the banks of the Tennessee River. The way by the river was shorter, but people traveling along it could be seen by the soldiers on guard in the Southern camp.

General Rosecrans thought the Southern general would expect him to take the valley road. He decided, however, to use the road by the river. He knew his men might be caught as they were bringing supplies to camp. Therefore, he put General Burnside on one side of the river with thousands of soldiers and General Crook, also with thousands, on the other side. General Burnside's men were to fight the Southern soldiers if they tried to cross the river.

General Wheeler's men rode up and began firing at Burnside's men. After the Northern soldiers had been driven back, Wheeler crossed the river at a ford. Crook's men fought the Southern soldiers as they reached the other side of the river. "Fighting Joe" rode up and down the lines, cheering his men and calling to them to come on and drive Crook away. They went on. They drove Crook and his men away. They cut off the Northern soldiers from their supplies. Seven thousand mules and twelve hundred wagons filled with food and other supplies were captured.

General Sherman, a great Northern general, afterward said: "In case of war with a foreign country, General Joseph Wheeler should be put in command of the cavalry of the United States." Many years after the War Between the States ended, General Wheeler fought in another war. He went to Cuba to fight in the Spanish-American War. He was sixty-two years old, but he was just as brave as ever.

Once during the Spanish-American War, General Wheeler wished to find out something about a part of the Spanish army which was in front of him. He would not send his men, because they would be in great danger; the enemy would be sure to see them and fire at them. So he went alone and climbed into a tree in order to get a better view. He found out all he wished to learn and got down safely before the enemy could shoot him.

General Wheeler was called on to help command the military, and he did so well enough that the Americans won the victory. Now you see why he was called a hero of two wars.

When General Wheeler was not fighting, he was helping his state and his country in other ways. He was at all times a valuable citizen.

Just across the Potomac River from Washington there is a beautiful cemetery called Arlington. It is the National Cemetery. Many of our brave men are buried there; among them is General Joe Wheeler. A tall monument marks the place where this true soldier lies. We remember him as one of Alabama's greatest men.

Hobson and His Brave Companions

Now we will discuss another interesting story in which an Alabamian did his part for the United States. The setting was the Spanish-American War. Remember this war was fought with Spain, the country from which Columbus and De Soto came to America. It was the second war in which Joe Wheeler served.

Cuba was owned by Spain. Cuba is our nearest neighbor to the south. Cuba was in trouble. Soldiers from Spain were mistreating the Cubans, who were starving. They begged the United States to help them.

The Spanish Admiral, Cervera (Ser-ve-ra), brought the finest warships of Spain to Cuba. They anchored in Santiago Bay. The land is very close on each side of the entrance to the harbor where Cervera had his ships, leaving little room for a vessel sailing in or out.

"Ah," said Admiral Sampson, one of our commanders, "let's catch them in the harbor! Let's keep them from coming out."

A secret meeting was held by the officers of the American fleet to make a plan to catch the Spanish ships in the harbor. Among those at the meeting was a young man from Alabama, Richmond Pearson Hobson, who suggested a fine plan.

This was the plan: A United States ship was to run into the harbor. Just as it reached the narrow part of the entrance, the sailors on board were to blow it up, so that it would sink crosswise in the channel. Thus, it would be in the way of the Spanish ships when they tried to get out. Then the Americans would have the Spanish ships trapped in the harbor, unable to escape.

The Spaniards had towers from which they watched the harbor and its entrance. The moment the American ship entered the channel, they would fire on it and sink it, and all the sailors would be lost. If the men were not shot by the Spaniards or drowned, it seemed certain that they would be killed when they blew up their own vessel!

Three thousand men were told of the plan. "Who will offer to go as commander of the ship?" the question was asked. "I will," said Lieutenant Hobson. When it was asked who would go with Lieutenant Hobson, every man of the three thousand offered. But only seven could be taken. In the darkness of the night, Lieutenant Hobson and his seven companions sailed away in the Merrimac.

Bang! Bang! Boomed the Spanish guns as the Merrimac came into sight. Bravely the ship plowed through the waves, although the Spaniards had shot off her steering wheel. Suddenly the Spaniards heard a loud "Boom!" Then they saw bits of the American ship flying toward the sky. Down sank the hull of the Merrimac, and the Spanish fleet was nearly shut up in the harbor. Only a small outlet was left open. Lieutenant Hobson and his men were plunged into the cold, dark water.

At daybreak, Cervera, the Spanish admiral, found them clinging to a raft. His boat came close to the raft, and our brave sailors climbed aboard it as prisoners. Not one of them was hurt. Cervera took them to the fort at the entrance to the harbor, fed and warmed them, and was kind to them. He admired their bravery.

Afterward Cervera sent sailors to the American ships with a white flag. This white flag meant that the Americans were not to fire on the Spaniards, but to listen to a message. The white flag is called a flag of truce.

The Spanish sailors brought glad news. It made a mother and a sister in Alabama cry for joy, for Lieutenant Hobson was safe. It made the families of the other brave men happy too. Admiral Cervera promised to exchange the sailors for Spanish prisoners the Americans had taken. After the war was over, the courageous soldiers came back to their homes in the United States. Lieutenant Hobson was promoted to the rank of captain in the navy.

One Sunday while the American admiral was away, the Spaniards tried to take their ships out of the harbor. The Spaniards thought no one was watching. They tried in vain. Only one of their vessels could pass the sunken Merrimac at a time. This meant that they were delayed until the American ships arrived. A fight took place in which all the Spanish ships were captured, the brave Admiral Cervera with them.

Spain found out that we knew how to help Cuba. The United States drove the Spaniards out of Cuba, which became a free country. This is what Captain Hobson said about heroism: "Heroism is found in all lands, in all times. Its basic element is self-sacrificing love." The Bible tells us: "Greater love hath no man than this that a man lay down his life for a friend."

CHAPTER 14
WOMEN OF COURAGE

Vocabulary:

Braille
Stupidity
Infinite
Preparatory
Progressive
Anticipation
Opportunity

Handicap
Freedom
Destiny
Excellent
Recitations
Discrimination

Genius
Patient
Equality
Character
Education
Reputation

Research Suggestions:

1. What other things has Julia Tutwiler written? What interesting things can you learn about her and her writing?

2. Did Julia Tutwiler marry and have children of her own?

3. How did Helen Keller become blind?

4. Why was Miss Sullivan so committed to teaching Helen?

5. What schools did Helen attend?

6. Who invented Braille? How and why did Braille become a written language?

7. Jesse & Frank James visited North Alabama during the year of 1881. What interesting things occurred in Alabama that they were blamed for?

People & Places to Research:

Condoleezza Rice	Emmylou Harris	Tammy Wynette
Howard Weeden	Helen Keller	Anne Mathilde Bilbro
Florence Golson Bateman	Miss Annie Sullivan	Maud Lindsay

Watch publisher's website BWPublications.com for Maud Lindsay's books.

Science & Nature Study

1. Research the following plants & birds:

Blue Jay	Chickadee	Brown Creeper
House Wren	Mockingbird	Tobacco
Red-Winged Blackbird	Butterfly weed	Wild Hyacinth
Echinacea or Purple Cone Flower		

2. Research the five senses:
Hearing, Sight, Taste, Touch, Smell

Project Suggestions:

1. Write a poem about Alabama or your hometown. Add this to your *Alabama Timeline Journal Notebook*.

2. Start your own magazine or newsletter. It could be something you send out to relatives that live out of town. Have everyone in the family write something for the newsletter.

Dramatization Suggestion:

Dramatize a scene from Helen Keller's life.

Map Work:

Mark Tuscumbia on your map.

Local & Family History:

Go to your local library's genealogy room and look up information about your city/county and family. Call your grandparents and older family members to learn what you can about the family.

1. Create a newspaper. Each member of your family could write an article, creating a scenario from the year your newspaper will be published.

A Tiny Poet

Not all little girls can read before they are five years old. In little Julia Tutwiler's home, her brothers and sisters read through their primers before they were five. When Julia's fifth birthday came near without her being able to read, her mother began to worry because she had not done as well as the other children. She talked to little Julia, and the tiny girl tried harder. She tried so hard that she learned to read in a very short time.

Julia grew to love reading so much that she wanted to read the books in her father's library. Before she was six years old, she had read many of them. Julia thought everyone should be taught to read. She even chased her baby sister all about the house, holding out her primer, trying to teach the baby to read.

There were beautiful poems in the books in the Tutwiler library which Julia enjoyed. She memorized some of them and tried to put her own pretty thoughts into poems. One day, after the sun had set, Julia's brothers and sisters were out on the steps talking. She was missing and they were guessing where she was. Just then the little girl opened the garden gate and came in. She had pushed off her sunbonnet, but it hung on behind by the strings tied under her chin. She held a paper in her hand and she looked so happy that her mother asked, "Where have you been, Julia?"

"In the peach orchard, Mother, writing a poem," answered the child.

"Tell us about it, Julia," begged the other children.

Julia gave the paper to her mother. How the children enjoyed hearing her read the little poem Julia had written about the sunset! Her mother said it was very good for a six-year-old girl to have written.

> **Timeline**
>
> **1886-1890**
> Thomas Seay is the governor of the state of Alabama.
>
> **1886**
> Montgomery has the first electric street cars in the South.
>
> **1886**
> Hugo Black is born in Clay County, Alabama.
>
> **1889-1893**
> Benjamin Harrison is President of the United States.
>
> **1889**
> Joseph Wheeler serves again as U.S. Congressman from Alabama.

> **Timeline**
>
> **1890-1894**
> Thomas G. Jones is the governor of the state of Alabama.
>
> **1893-1897**
> Grover Cleveland is President of the United States, 2nd term.
>
> **1893**
> Margaret Murray Washington marries Booker T. Washington.
>
> **1893**
> Women are admitted to the University of Alabama.

Julia wrote many other poems. One poem that she wrote when she was only nine years old was published in a magazine.

There were not as many magazines back then as there are now. Julia thought she would enjoy running a magazine of her own. She asked one of her sisters to help her get a magazine started. The children had no way to print a magazine, so they wrote it with a pen.

Once a month the sisters published their magazine called *The Monthly Rose*. It was written in three columns on blue paper. Julia wrote stories and poems for it. The sisters gathered all the funny sayings they could find and read this part of the magazine to the black children on the place. The Tutwiler children were very kind to the small black children. Julia also wrote little plays, which her brothers and sisters and cousins helped her to perform.

Several miles from the Tutwiler home there lived some poor children who could not go to school because there wasn't a school nearby. Julia thought they should have the opportunity to learn. Although she was only fifteen years old, she made up her mind to teach them. She believed anyone who could not read was not a good citizen. Besides, people who could not read missed out on the pleasure that the Tutwiler children found in reading.

The only way for the girl to get to the poor children was by riding horseback over rough, lonely roads. Everyday she took one of her brothers on her horse with her, and they galloped to her school. Julia Tutwiler taught the whole school. She said that one little boy at the school knew the multiplication tables without having to study them. This boy grew up to be a fine citizen. Julia was proud of all of the children of her school.

Just as she tried to teach her baby sister and rode far to teach other children who could not go to school, in later years Julia spent her life helping to educate boys and girls of Alabama. She planned and talked about schools for girls, such as she had seen for boys. She raised money for schools, and she taught in some of them.

Miss Tutwiler thought that even girls in prison should be taught. She visited them in prisons and in places where they worked and helped to make their lives better. After one of her visits to a prison some one said, "God has sent an angel to us. Miss Tutwiler was here yesterday and today's work is in the sunshine."

Miss Tutwiler was the woman that wrote our state song, *"Alabama"*.

When you sing the words of the state song *"Alabama,"* think of how Miss Julia Tutwiler loved our state.

Alabama
Written by Julia S. Tutwiler

Alabama, Alabama
We will aye be true to thee,
From thy Southern shores where groweth.
By the sea thy orange tree
To thy Northern vale where floweth,
Deep blue the Tennessee
Alabama, Alabama, we will aye be true to thee.
Broad thy stream whose name thou bearest,
Grand thy Bigbee rolls along
Fair thy Coosa-Tallapoosa,
Bold thy Warrior dark and strong.
Goodlier than the land that Moses
Climbed lone Nebb's Mount to see.
Alabama, Alabama, we will aye be true to thee.
Brave and pure thy men and women,
Better this than corn and wine
Make us worthy, God in Heaven
Of this goodly land of Thine.

Hearts as open as thy doorways.
Liberal hands and spirits free.
Alabama, Alabama, we will aye be true to thee.
Little, little can I give thee,
Alabama, mother mine.
But that little - hand, brain, spirit.
All I have and am are thine.
Take, O take, the gift and giver.
Take and serve thyself with me.
Alabama, Alabama, we will aye be true to thee.

The Story of Helen Keller

Everybody who comes to Tuscumbia, Alabama, goes to see an old-fashioned frame house in a yard with magnolias, crêpe myrtle, and other beautiful Southern plants. But they don't visit to see these things; they actually wish to see the office in the yard, a cottage with roses growing over the porch. For in this office Helen Keller was born. Helen Keller, the daughter of Captain and Mrs. Arthur Keller, lived a fascinating life, full of courage.

Until Helen was nineteen months old, she was a happy, healthy baby walking and learning to talk like other babies. Then she had a terrible illness with a high fever, day after day for many days. When she grew better, her brother, Jimmie, tried to amuse her by dangling his watch in front of her. She had always loved to hold the watch and put it to her ears to hear it tick, but now she did not notice it. "I believe there is something wrong with Helen's eyes!" he said. This was only too true. She was blind, and not only blind, but deaf as well! Be-

Birthplace of Helen Keller

cause she was deaf, she lost her ability to understand sound, which resulted in a loss of speech.

Of course, she did not understand what had happened to her. Her world, which had been sunshine and laughter, was now always dark, always silent. Slowly, she learned how to make herself understand, for she had a bright mind and a strong, active body. She followed her mother around by holding to her dress. She would push or pull the way she wished to go. She quickly learned that if she kicked and cried, she could get her own way; her parents felt so sorry for her that they could not bear to have her cry.

Nobody in those days thought of going out without a hat or bonnet, and children wore sunbonnets to keep their complexions clear and white. One day, when Helen was three years old, she was to take a ride with "Aunt Ev" (Miss Evelyn Keller) in her surrey. When her bonnet was tied on, she snatched it off and threw it down. As fast as it was put on, she threw it off. Then she ran and found the nurse and pulled at the bandanna the nurse wore on her head. They got a handkerchief, tied knots in it just like those in her nurse's head kerchief and put it on Helen. This was what she wanted. She went to ride perfectly satisfied and wore a bandanna every time she went out for the rest of that summer. Helen was very proud of what she thought were pretty clothes. She liked ruffles and would feel to see if her dress was ruffled.

She was a great pet of Aunt Ev's and would often stay with her. Whatever Helen wanted, Aunt Ev did. Once Helen awoke in the middle of the night, demanded that she get up, dress, and have her breakfast. You must remember that day and night were the same to Helen. Aunt Ev dressed her, cooked breakfast, and began another day at midnight.

Helen was mischievous. One day, she locked her mother up in a closet and then sat on the steps and laughed. Mrs. Keller called and knocked and banged on the door. Helen could not hear her, and it was sometime before anyone else did.

Helen had a little black playmate named Martha Washington. Martha Washington's wooly hair was wrapped in tight knots all over her head. Helen's hair hung in golden curls. One day, while they were seated on the back steps cutting paper dolls, Helen snipped off one of Martha Washington's knots. Martha Washington in turn cut off one of Helen's curls. Perhaps they would have snipped and cut all of the hair off each other's heads if Mrs. Keller had not seen what they were doing and put a stop to their barbering.

Helen loved pets. She had a cockatoo, a white Persian cat, and several dogs. Black Beauty was her pony, Neddy was her donkey, and Wade was her horse. She would sniff when one of them came near and could tell them by their smell. She loved to feed the chickens, to hunt for hen's nests and eggs and to go with the cook when she milked the cow. She enjoyed petting the cow and would carry her cup along for a drink of warm milk.

Her best-loved doll was a rag doll named Nancy. Poor Nancy led a hard life; Helen threw her down anywhere when she grew tired of her. In fact, Helen was so hard on her playthings that her mother had special doll furniture made for her that she could not break.

Helen's parents had read of Laura Bridgeman, who was deaf, dumb, and blind. Yet, Laura had learned to read and write. They wrote to Perkins Institute for the Blind and asked about a teacher for Helen. The Perkins Institute sent Miss Annie Sullivan to Tuscumbia, Alabama to work with young Helen. Miss Annie Sullivan began by spelling the word 'doll' on Helen's hand and putting Nancy in her arms. She did this over and over until Helen knew that the signs made on her hand meant her doll. She made the signs herself and was overjoyed. After she had learned a good many words, her teacher took her to the pump and let water run over her hand. Then she spelled water. For the first time, it dawned on Helen that everything had a name. After this, she was taught to read by feeling words written in raised letters on cardboard.

Although Helen had no trouble learning to talk on her fingers and to read, she was still disobedient. If she could not do as she pleased, she would fly into a tantrum. Miss Sullivan was in despair. She told Captain and Mrs. Keller that she must have Helen away from the rest of the family if she was to teach her. This was hard for Helen's parents, for they did not have the heart to control Helen themselves. They were sensible, however, and made plans for Miss Sullivan to have Helen to herself.

Furniture that Helen had never known was put into the office and in the yard and everything was made comfortable. Helen's father drove her around in his buggy in several directions and then put her over the fence so that she would not know where she was. Aunt Ev was to send Miss Sullivan and Helen's meals to them in the office.

Helen nor her teacher were altogether happy. For the first time in her life, Helen could not do exactly as she pleased. One morning at ten o'clock, Captain Keller came through the garden and peeped in the window. There was Helen in her nightgown, sitting on the floor, the picture of woe. Miss Sullivan would not give Helen her breakfast until she dressed. Miss Sullivan held out, and Helen had to give in. Soon she began to understand that she must obey, and then she became loving and happy.

As much as possible, she lived like other children. Helen loved to read. Her cousin, Leila Keller, tells about one night when the rest of the family was sitting in the brightly lit hall playing cards and Helen was in a dark bedroom reading. Some one had sent her a copy of Black Beauty written in Braille. She had been reading all day, and her little fingers were so pricked that they left a trail of blood across each line. Her cousin Leila did not like for Helen to be in the dark room all alone; so she went in and said, "Helen, don't sit in this dark by yourself. Come out into the hall with us."

"Cousin Leila," Helen answered, "my spirit is never in the dark. It is always in the light." She was only ten years old!

It was when she was ten that she first heard that deaf children learned to understand what people said by watching the movement of their lips and learned to talk by moving their lips in the same way. She was blind, but still she believed that her fingers could take the place of her eyes and that through them she too could learn to understand and talk. Her teacher and her parents feared that she would fail and be greatly disappointed. Helen was not the kind to give up. So they had a special teacher to see what could be done for her. Soon Helen began to understand the spoken word and to talk.

This was very hard for her, but she slowly improved. She could not hear; so her voice did not sound natural, but she would speak very carefully, and people could learn to understand her. If you were talking to Helen, she would place her forefinger on your lips. You would have to speak slowly and distinctly. Helen would then pronounce each word after you and then answer you.

Helen Keller went through college with other students. She made no excuses for herself because of her handicaps. She became a very brilliant and respected woman. She spoke before some of the most famous people of her time. She also wrote about many interesting things. Her heart went out to the deaf and blind; and she helped them, not only with money, but by helping other people see the need for educating the handicapped.

She received the Pictorial Review's annual $5,000 gift for the greatest work accomplished in the year 1931. This great work was the completion of the first million-dollar fund for the American Foundation for the Blind.

It is not only the blind and deaf whom Helen Keller helped, however, for her beautiful courage was and still is a great lesson to us all. H. G. Wells, a well-known English writer, once said: "Helen Keller is the greatest person living in the world today."

Here is an invitation to a party written by Helen to her little friend Maud Lindsay.

Here is another letter:

January
Tuscumbia, Alabama.

Dear Maud,
I am glad to write to you. I am going to Boston in June. I will have fun with blind girls. I will be eight years old. I came to see Bell. Minnie Lindsay and Mattie Lindsay are here.

Goodbye,
Helen Keller

The women of Alabama that we have covered in this study are just a few of the many incredible women that have played a part in the history of our great state. Please make sure you go through the timeline as well as the research suggestions at the beginning of the chapter and research more about women in the history of Alabama.

CHAPTER 15
WORLD WARS

Vocabulary:

Allies	Armistice	Co-operate
Submarines	Periscope	Torpedo
Register	Questionnaire	Draft
Secretary of War	Camouflage	Destroyer
Code	Vital	

Research Suggestions:

1. Are there members of your family or people in your community who fought in World War I or World War II? What was their job? How did their service during the war affect their life after the war?

2. What are some of the organizations from Alabama that helped during these wars?

3. During World War II, Alabama began manufacturing many different items. What are some of these items? How were these items used for the war effort?

4. During these war times many women left their homes and went to work in factories. Why did this happen?

People & Places to Research:

Lt. William C. Maxwell
Tuskegee Airmen of World War II
Wright Brother's Flight into Alabama
Tallulah Bankhead
Arthur George Gaston
William Christopher Handy

The World War - The Army

After the Spanish-American War was over, it was hoped that the United States would never have to go to war again. But in 1917, we felt that we must take part in a war that had been going on in Europe for almost three years. England and France and their allies had been fighting Germany and her allies. Germany had built many ships called submarines which sailed underwater. Although the submarines sailed under the sea, they were able to see ships through a long tube called a periscope. When a submarine saw an enemy ship, it would shoot a torpedo at the ship and sink it.

Although we were not in the war at first, Germany tried to keep us from trading with England and France and their allies. We said that we had a right to trade with anybody we pleased. When Germany sank some of our ships, we became very angry. When Germany refused to stop, the United States said that Germany was waging war on us. We entered the World War on the side of England and France.

When a war is being fought, everybody in the country gets very busy. First, there must be soldiers. It was decided that every man in the United States between the ages of twenty-one and thirty-one must sign his name in a book called a register. Soldiers were drawn from these registers. On registration day, the men marched to the nearest registration center. The United States flag was held high before them while the band played *"America"* and *"The Star Spangled Banner"*. The school children, the teachers, and many other citizens marched in the procession, and the mothers of the registering men rode in cars.

As the men registered, they had to answer a list of questions called a questionnaire. These questionnaires asked many things; their color, their work, how many years they had gone to school, whether they were married or single, whether they had any children, and

---

Timeline

1894-1896
William C. Oates is the governor of the state of Alabama.

1895
The state flag is adopted by legislature.

1896
The state's first hydroelectric power plant is built on Tallapoosa River.

1896-1900
Joseph F. Johnston is the governor of the state of Alabama.

whether they had any disease or not. This questionnaire also asked if the young man was in college.

The blacks were put into black companies, and the whites into white companies. Those who had been in automobile repair shops, for instance, would do their best service by taking care of the army cars, trucks, and machines of various kinds. Those who were too delicate to fight might work in government offices. Young men that were not in college were called before the men who were in college. Alabama was such a poor area in the south that we had a high number of young men that were not in college. Therefore, we had a large number of young men called to serve our country. Married men with children were to be called last.

There was a number opposite each name registered. All of these numbers were put into capsules and placed in a large glass bowl. Secretary of War Newton D. Baker drew out the first capsule. This was called the first draft. That meant that the men whose numbers had been drawn must be the first to go to training camps to be trained to fight.

> **Timeline**
>
> **1897-1901**
> William McKinley is President of the United States.
>
> **1900**
> Donald Croom Beatty is born in Birmingham, Alabama.
>
> **1900-June 1901**
> William J. Samford is the governor of the state of Alabama. He died in office.
>
> **October 16, 1901**
> Booker T. Washington visits President Theodore Roosevelt at the White House.
>
> **1901**
> Yet another new constitution is written in Montgomery.

The World War the Navy

We needed not only an army, but a navy as well. We needed a navy because we had to take our men overseas to fight in France. We had to send food, clothing, and war supplies to them and to our allies. We had to protect our coasts and fight on the sea. Of course, Germany was on the lookout to sink our ships, so we painted them all sorts of colors in all sorts of ways. We did this to make it harder for the enemy to tell the difference between ships riding the waves and the waves themselves. We have a word for this—camouflage.

> **Timeline**
>
> **1901-1907**
> Willaim D. Jelks is the governor of the state of Alabama for 26 days.
>
> **1901-1909**
> Theodore Roosevelt is President of the United States.
>
> **September 15, 1902**
> Dr. Luther Hill of Montgomery performed a surgery to sew up the beating heart of a young man that was stabbed. The surgery was performed in the home of the victim. This was the first successful surgery of this kind ever performed.
>
> **February 9, 1903**
> Houston County, Alabama is established, being named in honor of Governor George S. Houston.

It was always a secret when our ships were to sail. A number would go together and small speedy war vessels called destroyers would go with them to look out for submarines and sink them. Instead of moving straight along their path on the ocean as ships usually do, our ships zigzagged to puzzle the enemy about which way they were going. To do this safely, the boats always had to keep the same distance apart. At night, not a light could be seen on the ships. All of this made crossing the sea very dangerous. The destroyers would go out with the ships a few hundred miles and then return to shore because there was not so much danger of submarines on the high seas. Then our government would send word in a secret code across the sea that our ships were on the way. When it was near the time for our ships to reach Europe, destroyers on that side would come out to meet them and escort them to a harbor.

Life on a destroyer was hard and dangerous. These ships not only had to look out for submarines, but they also had to be careful not to get in the way of our own zig-zagging ships.

The little destroyers were made for speed and could not carry a large water tank. So the supply of water was small. The officers in charge of a destroyer had to be very strict about the sailors' wasting drinking water. Here is an order that was given on the destroyer Decatur:

November 19, 1917

NOTICE

WATER

REGULATION OF FRESH WATER ISSUE

1. The man who takes or wastes one drop of fresh water will, in a case like this, be a traitor to his shipmates and a menace to the lives of all.

Daily Issue

1. Water for drinking as needed.

1. At 9:00 A. M. every second day—2 quarts of water for washing and cleaning. Fresh water will not be issued or used for the following purposes; washing dishes; washing clothes (unless part of the two-quart issue); making soups; boiling potatoes or bathing (except the two-quart issue.)

2. It is suggested that two, three, or four, who may chum together, pool their water for bathing and afterward for washing clothes. This is not a new idea, but one that has been practiced in years past.

1. I cannot too strongly impress upon the crew the vital necessity of every man's cooperation to save every drop of fresh water. Otherwise, we will never reach the other side, or if we do reach it, the ship will be in such condition as to be surveyed unfit for duty.

2. Don't throw away a drop, save it for washing.

H. A. McClure, Commanding Officer

> **Timeline**
>
> **1904**
> Helen Keller of Tuscumbia becomes the first deaf and blind person to graduate from college.
>
> **1904-1905**
> Russell M. Cunningham acts as governor of the state of Alabama while Governor Jelks was ill.
>
> **1906**
> Alabama Power is incorporated.
>
> **1907-1911**
> Braxton Bragg Comer is the governor of the state of Alabama.

The World War Life in America

Not only were the men to go to war, but everybody had to help to win the war. There had to be money, so there were taxes on picture show tickets and on all sorts of other pleasures, on things to eat and things to drink—on almost everything.

There had to be food, not only for our own soldiers, but also for our allies who had fought for so long. No white flour was allowed to be sold. Other grain had to be used with wheat flour; wheat flour was needed for the army. This made the bread dark; it was called 'war bread.'

> **Timeline**
>
> **1909**
> Mobile establishes a 10:00 P.M. curfew for black people.
>
> **1909-1913**
> William H. Taft is President of the United States.
>
> **1911-1915**
> Emmet O'Neal is the governor of the state of Alabama.
>
> **March 23, 1912**
> Wernher von Braun is born in Wirzitz, Germany.
>
> **1913-1921**
> Woodrow Wilson is President of the United States.

Hotels and public eating-places were told to observe Monday and Wednesday as wheatless days, Tuesday as meatless day, Saturday as porkless day, and to serve one wheatless meal and one meatless meal every day. Two ounces of war bread were all one might eat at any meal, but one might have corn bread. Why? Cornmeal does not keep on sea voyages as well as wheat flour, so we could not ship it to our soldiers in Europe. Sugar was allowed for tea or coffee.

Merchants were asked not to heat their stores on Monday, which was heatless day. They were also asked not to use their electric signs except on Thursday and Saturday nights. The other nights were lightless nights. People were asked not to drive cars on Sunday, which was gasless day. Everybody was asked to wear old clothing and to lend money to the United States. Almost everybody did just what he was asked. Why? Because everybody loved his country and felt that the United States must win the war.

We wanted to help our soldiers and those of our allies as much as possible, so everybody joined the Red Cross. The members of the Red Cross sewed, made bandages, and knitted socks and sweaters for the soldiers; some went over to France to help take care of the men behind the trenches. The Knights of Columbus, The Y. M. C. A., The Y. W. C. A., The Y. M. H. A., and the Salvation Army all helped in many ways. We also had field hospitals farther back, where there was little danger that the enemy would come.

The First American Hero of the World War

A short time after our men began fighting in France, the newspapers came out with a headline in the tall black letters, F. A. H. These letters stood for First American Hero. This First American Hero was registered at the Florence, Alabama, Courthouse. His name was Homer Givens.

Homer Givens was a corporal who had been sent with four other men to a listening post to find out what the Germans were planning to do. After these five men had been hidden in a shell hole under fire for forty minutes, the Germans came "over the top." Four of the men in the hole ran and were captured. Homer Givens stood his ground and killed three Germans before he was wounded by a German bomb, trampled underfoot and left for dead. Later, he was carried to one of our army hospitals. Twenty-three pieces of shell were found in his body, yet his life was saved.

France gave Homer Givens a Croix de Guerre, a medal with which she honors her own great heroes. General Pershing, who was the head of our army in France, was present when Homer Givens received the Croix de Guerre. They tried to send Givens home, but he said, "I'm not going until I get even with the Huns."

Givens' Croix de Guerre was sent to his father. Major Simmons, an officer from Washington, brought it to Florence. All of Florence gathered at Coffee High School to show honor to her hero.

This message was sent to Homer Givens from Florence:

"With pride and gratitude your home and native land celebrate today, in honor of your heroism. Your Croix de Guerre was presented to your father by Major Simmons at a splendid gathering today. God's blessing upon you and the cause for which you battle. We keep the home fires burning." – *Florence Times News*

> **Timeline**
>
> **February 4, 1913**
> Rosa Parks is born Rosa Louise McCauley in Tuskegee, Alabama.
>
> **September 12, 1913**
> Jesse Owens is born in Oakville, Alabama.
>
> **November 14, 1915**
> Booker T. Washington dies. He is buried on the Tuskegee University campus grounds in a tomb hand built by the students.
>
> **1915-1919**
> Charles Henderson is the governor of the state of Alabama.

After The War

After the United States had fought for over a year, the "Allies" won the war. On the eleventh day of the eleventh month of 1918, at eleven o'clock in the morning, orders were

> **Timeline**
>
> **March 24, 1916**
> Julia Tutwiler dies of cancer.
>
> **1919-1923**
> Thomas E. Kilby is the governor of the state of Alabama.
>
> **1920**
> First rural electric lines are run in Madison County.
>
> **July 4, 1920**
> William Crawford Gorgas dies in London, England. He is buried in Arlington Cemetery in Virginia.

given by both sides to stop fighting. This was called an Armistice. You can imagine how happy everybody on the winning side was. In Alabama and everywhere else whistles blew, bells rang, bands played, flags waved in the air, people stopped work, schools closed, and everybody was on the streets, talking, laughing, shaking hands and singing war songs.

Although, we were so happy on November 11, 1918, Armistice Day, we were sad too; for some of our men would never come back. If you will look at the monuments of this war in any town or city, you will see a long list of names of soldiers who died either in camp or in battle. As time passes, the world not only sees more and more how horrible war is, but we also feel the aftershock of war.

Someone has said that war is the greatest liar in the world. This is his proof: "War tells us that his sounds are hurrahs, songs, and bands playing gay marches. But the true sounds of war are the whining of bullets, the thunder of guns, the cries of pain, the groans of the dying, and the sobs of parents and widows and orphans for their dead. War tells us that his colors are gay flags, bright uniforms, polished swords, and guns glittering in the sun; but the true colors of war are the colors of mud, filth, and blood."

Most of the money that our people give to the United States goes to pay for wars we have fought or those we may have yet to fight. In what better ways might this money be spent if we knew we would never have to fight again?

A General Who Saved Millions of Lives: William Crawford Gorgas

William Crawford Gorgas was born on an Alabama plantation in 1854. His father, Josiah Gorgas, was an officer in the United States army. His mother, Amelia Gayle Gorgas, was the daughter of Governor John Gayle of Alabama.

When he was a little fellow, his parents moved to Charleston, South Carolina. While there, he must have heard talk of Southern rights and secession, but he was too young to understand it. He heard the first gun fired in the War Between the States. He saw the flag of South Carolina waving everywhere, and later the Confederate flag. No doubt, he sang *Dixie* and *Wait for the Wagon*.

General Josiah Gorgas was from the North and was an officer in the United States army. He must have found it hard to decide what he ought to do, but he made up his mind to join the Confederate army. President Davis put him in charge of war supplies such as guns, cannons, and ammunition.

General Gorgas Home

The Gorgas family moved next to Richmond, Virginia. At that time Richmond was the capitol of the Confederate States. In Richmond, Willie Gorgas heard of little other than war. Soldiers in gray, led by gallant officers, marched through the streets as they left for the army. The band played *Dixie* and *The Girl I Left Behind Me*.

After a while, life changed; the brilliant parade was over. Numbers of wounded men were in the hospitals, and men with only one leg or one arm sat on benches in the parks. People did not have enough food, and it was hard to get clothing.

When the war ended, the Gorgas family, like most other Southerners, was poor. In the course of time, General Josiah Gorgas, was bestowed with the honor of President of the

University of Alabama and moved to Tuscaloosa. William wanted to become a soldier, but failed to get an appointment to West Point. He determined to study medicine and enter the army as a surgeon. He succeeded in doing so.

Yellow fever was a much-dreaded disease in those days. When there was one case of fever in a place, very soon, there were others. It would spread like wildfire. Many of the people who became infected with yellow fever died. Business houses closed and there was great suffering and distress.

Nobody knew the cause of yellow fever or how to cure it. People would tie bags of asafetida around their necks, chew onions, and wear sponges soaked in vinegar tied over their mouths, hoping to escape the disease. Still they became sick and died. The fever always lasted until the fall frost. Then it would die out and perhaps would not return for some years.

Dr. Walter Reed believed that yellow fever was caused by the bite of the stegomyia mosquito that had first bitten a person ill with the disease. Dr. William Gorgas at first doubted this, but later decided that it was true. Now the question was, "How to get rid of the stegomyia?" During the Spanish-American War, large numbers of soldiers died of yellow fever. Mosquitoes swarmed everywhere in Cuba. What could be done? It became Dr. Gorgas' duty to find out.

It was learned that the stegomyia lived on human blood and that it was dainty and liked clean water in which to lay its eggs. Dr. Gorgas forbid any standing water around a house. There must be no vases of flowers and cisterns must be sealed over. Then he set traps for the stegomyia. He filled pans with nice clean water and after the stegomyia had laid its eggs in them, Dr. Gorgas would have oil poured on top of the water. What good would that do? The mosquito eggs would hatch into wiggle tails (little black, threadlike worms that wiggle about in the water) and come up to the surface to breathe. If the surface was covered with oil, the wiggle tails could not get air and they died. In time, there were no more stegomyia mosquitoes in Cuba and no more yellow fever!

When the United States wanted to build the Panama Canal so that ships could sail from the Atlantic to the Pacific without making the long trip around South America, it was necessary to get rid of both yellow fever and malarial fever in the Canal Zone. Both were so deadly that it was impossible to get the work done without the loss of an enormous number of lives. When Dr. Gorgas was put in charge of the health department, he destroyed the stegomyia mosquitoes in the same way as he had in Cuba; soon there was no more yellow fever.

But how was Dr. Gorgas to get rid of malarial fever, which was almost as deadly as yellow fever? There are hundreds of kinds of mosquitoes, but the doctors found out that only the anopheles mosquito carries malaria. The anopheles is not as dainty as the stegomyia, however, it likes to lay its eggs in stagnant pools and damp places under shrubbery. Although the anopheles does a great deal of flying about and singing, it does not fly farther from home than two hundred yards. When Dr. Gorgas found this out, he made people drain ponds, clean out gutters, cut down all shrubbery, and clear the land for two hundred yards from where they lived and worked. Of course, he had all the houses screened. After this, Panama became a healthy place to live and the great canal was built with very little loss of life.

When the United States entered the World War, General Gorgas was made Surgeon General of the United States Army. This meant that he had to plan camps and hospitals and look after all health conditions. By this time, he had become so well known and so highly respected, that nation after nation employed him to show them how to get rid of diseases.

In 1920, when General Gorgas was in London, getting ready to work in British West Africa, he became very ill. King George himself went to see him and showed him great honor.

William Crawford Gorgas died in London, July 4, 1920. The whole world mourned his death; a great service was held for him in St. Paul's Cathedral, London. The funeral procession was three miles long. His horse was led in the procession with his master's boots hung in reverse over the saddle; a custom in the army. His body was brought back to the United States in a special ship, and he was buried at Arlington. (Remember Arlington was General Lee's plantation home that the United States took during the War Between the States and made into a national cemetery, now known as Arlington Cemetery.)

When you go to see the University of Alabama at Tuscaloosa, be sure to see the old Gorgas home. It is kept in honor of General Josiah Gorgas, as former President of the University; of Amelia Gayle Gorgas, long time librarian of the university; and of William Crawford Gorgas, Alabama's great surgeon who helped save the world from much sickness, sorrow, and suffering.

CHAPTER 16
POWER GENERATION IN ALABAMA

Vocabulary:

Nitrates
Turbine
Energy

Explosives
Wisdom

Erect
Generator

Research Suggestions:

1. How many hydroelectric dams are in Alabama? Where are they located? What are the advantages of hydroelectric power over other sources of energy such as gas, oil, coal, and nuclear?

2. When did the construction of Wilson Dam begin? Where is it located? When was the dam completed? How have the hydroelectric dams throughout the state affected our state's economy?

3. Why did Henry Ford and Thomas Edison look into buying Wilson Dam?

4. Where was the first nuclear power plant built in Alabama? Who built it and when? How has this plant affected our economy and environment?

5. Research the New Deal. How much did it help Alabama?

6. Research Alabama Power Company. How is APC different from TVA?

People & Places to Research:

President Franklin D. Roosevelt
Idella Jones Childs
Willie Howard Mays

Alabama Power Company
Joe Louis

Science & Nature Study:

Research hydroelectric and nuclear energies.

Map Work:

Mark & Label the map with the different hydroelectric dams throughout Alabama.

Field Trip Suggestions:

Visit a hydroelectric dam in the state.

MUSCLE SHOALS

When the second World War was being fought, the United States needed nitrates to use in making explosives. Chemists had learned how to take nitrates from the air, but the machinery needed to secure these nitrates in large quantities required a great deal of power. What would be the best place to get this power?

For this purpose, a huge hydroelectric dam, (at that time the largest concrete building in the world), was erected at the foot of the Shoals and named Wilson Dam. Today the lovely lake sixteen miles long that is made by holding the water back is named Wilson Lake.

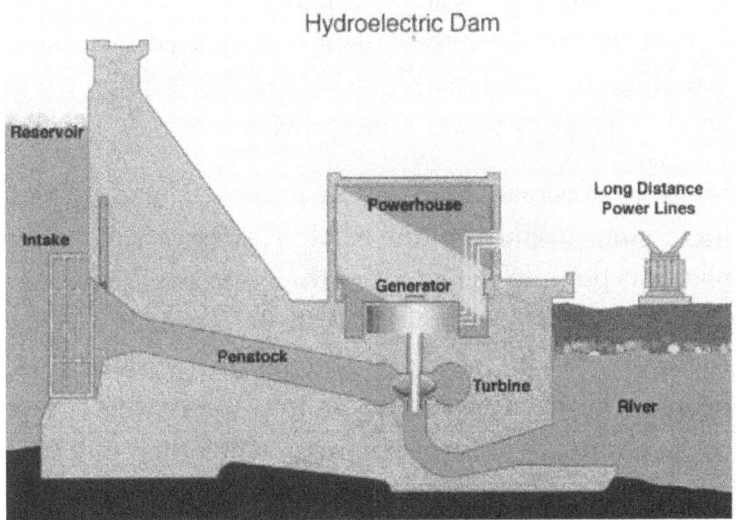

But how does a hydroelectric dam make electricity? Hydroelectric dams are different from other dams because they will have a hydroelectric generating unit inside the dam. The water on the upstream side of the dam will always be higher than the water on the downstream side of the dam. Water is allowed through the dam by a tunnel,

Timeline

1921-1923
Warren G. Harding is President of the United States.

1923-1927
William W. Brandon is the governor of the state of Alabama.

1923-1929
Calvin Coolidge is President of the United States.

1923
First long distance telephone line between Birmingham and Gadsden

1924
Charles S. McDowell, Lieutenant Governor, acts as governor for two days.

1925
Thomas Wesley Martin becomes president of Alabama Power Company serving until his death in 1964.

1925
Ku Klux Klan is resurrected and marches on Washington.

Timeline

1927-1931
Bibb Graves is the governor of the state of Alabama.

1928
W. C. Handy conducts a sixty-voice chorus and thirty-piece orchestra at Carnegie Hall.

1929-1933
Herbert C. Hoover is President of the United States.

1931-1935
Benjamin M. Miller is the governor of the state of Alabama.

1931
Nine black men are falsely accused of attacking two white women.

1933
Tennessee Valley Authority (TVA) is established to provide power, flood control and employment to the Tennessee Valley.

1933-1945
Franklin D. Roosevelt is President of the United States.

called a penstock. The penstock will direct the water to the turbine. The turbine is like a big propeller or pinwheel. The water flowing through the turbine will cause the turbine to spin, much as a pinwheel will turn when you blow on it. The turbine is connected to a generator, so when the turbine spins, the rotor in the generator will also spin. The spinning generator rotor causes the generator to produce electricity which is then carried to your home by power lines. So the next time you turn on your lights, some of the power used to light the light bulb may have come from a hydroelectric dam.

The war did not last as long as everyone feared that it would. For this reason, we did not need as many explosives. Nitrates are needed in making fertilizers as well as explosives. So, the nitrate plant can be used in time of peace. It took some years, however, to decide just what to do with the great power found at Muscle Shoals.

In 1933, President Franklin D. Roosevelt made a plan for the improvement of the whole Tennessee Valley. This plan was put into the hands of the Tennessee Valley Authority to be carried out. We call the Tennessee Valley Authority, "TVA" for short. Through the work of TVA, people who lived in villages and on farms would have cheap electricity to furnish lights, to cook their meals, to churn their milk, to wash and iron their clothes, to run their radios, to cool them in summer and warm them in winter. Do you remember how hard the pioneer women had to work? TVA changed the way things were done in the Tennessee Valley.

The TVA plan was not just to supply less expensive fertilizer for the farmers to grow better crops and cheaper power to run our factories. It was expected that our beautiful Tennessee Valley would become the garden spot of our country.

People came to Alabama from far and near to see Wilson Dam.

The New Deal

The New Deal was a plan to help Alabama and all of the rest of the United States. When President Franklin D. Roosevelt first became president, Alabama and the whole country was in the midst of a depression. People did not have any money to buy clothes; as a result the mills closed. Then the merchants could not sell goods. The iron mines closed because the owners could not sell iron. Many banks failed and people lost the money that they had put into the bank for saving.

Men with families to care for were out of work. Young men and women just out of college could not find work. Millions of people were homeless and starving.

The New Deal helped the unemployed to become employed. It also helped the farmer keep his farm, and people everywhere to save their homes or build homes by lending them money and making it easy to pay it back. The thing you know about TVA is only a small part of the work the New Deal accomplished.

Franklin D. Roosevelt and the New Deal restored hope during the depression. When the time came to re-elect a president, millions of people voted to keep Franklin D. Roosevelt in office for another term.

Timeline

1935-1939
Bibb Graves is the governor of the state of Alabama. He was the first governor to serve two four-year terms.

1936
Jesse Owens wins 4 gold medals in the Olympics.

1937
Maria Fearing, after serving in Africa as a missionary, dies at the age of 94, a free woman on the same plantation where she was born a slave.

1937
Hugo Black is appointed to U.S. Supreme Court.

December 29, 1938
Construction begins on the Bankhead Tunnel in Mobile, Alabama. The tunnel ran under the Mobile River; construction was finished in 22 months.

Timeline

1939-1943
Frank M. Dixon is the governor of the state of Alabama.

1941
Tuskegee Airmen, serve with incredible record during WWII.

December 7, 1941
Pearl Harbor is bombed.

Alabama Power Company

William Patrick Lay, a third generation riverboat captain, dreamed of utilizing the Coosa River to generate power for Alabamians. Lay and his associates formed the Alabama Power Company in Gadsden, Alabama on December 4, 1906. They gained congressional approval to build a hydroelectric dam on the Coosa River near Lock 12. Unable to raise the financing necessary to build the dam, Lay sold his interest in Alabama Power in 1912 to James Mitchell, a Massachusetts businessman, who had spent the past 17 years bringing electricity to Brazil. A year later, Alabama sold its first electricity to 100 customers in Talladega. This power was generated from its newly acquired Jackson Shoals Plant. Alabama electric completed its first major hydroelectric plant on the Coosa River near Lock 12 in 1914. The dam was renamed Lay Dam in honor of Alabama Power's founder William Patrick Lay in 1929.

Alabama Power continued to grow throughout the years building additional hydroelectric dams, fossil power plants, and a nuclear power plant. They have also been active in helping to develop other industries in Alabama and improving education.

CHAPTER 17
CIVIL RIGHTS MOVEMENT

Copy Work:

"The unwelcomed, unwanted, unwarranted, and force-induced intrusion upon the campus of the University of Alabama today of the might of the central government offers frightful example of the oppression of the rights, privileges and sovereignty of this state by officers of the federal government." - George Wallace

Research Suggestions:

1. What is the Jim Crow Law? Research the history of the Jim Crow law? Add this into your *Alabama Timeline Journal Notebook*.

2. What was the free march? What did it have to do with black voters? What chain of events did the march throw into motion? Add this into your *Alabama Timeline Journal Notebook*.

3. Who was Rosa Parks? Write an essay about her life. Add this into your *Alabama Timeline Journal Notebook*.

4. Research Martin Luther King Jr. What did he accomplish in Alabama? Add your research into your *Alabama Timeline Journal Notebook*.

5. What is the NAACP? What does this group accomplish? What is their mission statement? Add this into your *Alabama Timeline Journal Notebook*.

6. What do you think the federal government could have done to stop the Jim Crow society in the South? Do you think this would have worked? Why or why not?

7. When were the public schools in your county desegregated?

8. Why did white Southerners believe that a separate code of laws applying only to "black persons" was necessary?

9. Do you think that the U.S. government should have confiscated lands owned by Confederate leaders to provide "40 acres and a mule" to the landless freedmen? Why or why not?

People & Places to Research:

Martin Luther King Jr.	Hugo L. Black	Jimmie Lee Jackson
Harper Lee	Nat King Cole	Rosa Parkers
George Wallace	National Guard	Ku Klux Klan
Segregation	James Cleveland Owens	Bus Boycotts
Church Bombing	Jim Crow Law	Tuskegee Airman

The Fight for Freedom

There was a time in Alabama when blacks and white people could not use the same restroom, eat in the same restaurant or drink from the same water fountain. At this point in time, black children and white children did not go to schools together. Everything was segregated, giving white citizens priority over black people in every situation.

When the Civil War ended, it left behind enormous unresolved problems.

The discrimination only became more prevalent from the end of the war up through the 1960's. Many factors contributed to the enabling of segregation for many years.

Share Cropping

At the end of the war, the South was full of unemployed people in need of work to provide the basic necessities for their families.

There was also a huge need for people to help work the farms and plantations that no longer had slave labor after the war ended.

> **Timeline**
>
> **1942**
> Wernher Von Braun launches his first V2 rocket in North Germany.
>
> **1943-1947**
> Chauncey M. Sparks is the governor of the state of Alabama.
>
> **January 5, 1943**
> George Washington Carver dies. He was buried beside Booker T. Washington on the Tuskegee Institute Campus. His tombstone reads: "He could have added fortune to fame, but caring for neither, he found happiness and honor in being helpful to the world."

It was at this time, sharecropping was established. In most cases the sharecropper was given a house to live in and credit at the general store with a high interest rate. When the crops were harvested, the general store was paid before the sharecropper received his portion of the crop money. In many cases, there was little to no cash delivered to the sharecropper, but if the crop was good his account at the general store was paid off so his family could purchase the things they need on credit once again at a high interest rate. There was a law established to protect the land owner; many refer to this as a "crop lien."

The freedmen, now sharecropping, were once again at the mercy of the white landowners.

Timeline

March 13, 1945
Martha Crystal Myers is born.

1945-1953
Harry S. Truman is President of the United States.

1947-1951
James E. Folsom is the governor of the state of Alabama.

1949
TVA begins building coal/steam plants to meet the growing demands for power in the Tennessee Valley.

Jim Crow Law

There was a strong, unspoken, separate but equal standard that was practiced all over the country but most strongly in the South. Some people called this the "Jim Crow Law." This was, of course, not a legislation voted on, but a Southern standard that no one dared to break for fear that their life, family's safety and reputation would be in jeopardy.

Most people who grew up in the South before 1960 knew the standard the black people were expected to uphold. This was a Southern etiquette that governed not only behavior, but manner and attitude as well. Blacks dare not break this practice of Southern protocol for fear of the retaliation that would come from the silent but sure gatekeepers of the old Southern traditions.

We are going to look at what some of the unspoken rules that were observed by those living in the South at this time. A black male could not offer his hand (to shake hands) with a white male because it implied being socially equal. Blacks and whites were not to eat together. If they did eat together, whites were to be served first, and some sort of partition to be placed between the races.

Jim Crow etiquette was that blacks were introduced to whites, never whites to blacks. Perhaps you would say: "Mr. Peters (the white person), this is Charlie (the black person), that I spoke to you about." Whites did not use courtesy titles of respect when referring to blacks, for example, Mr., Mrs., Miss., Sir, or Ma'am. Instead, blacks were called by their first names. Blacks had to use courtesy titles when referring to whites, and were not allowed to call them by their first names.

If a black person rode in a car driven by a white person, the black person sat in the back seat, or the back of a truck. White motorists had the right-of-way at all intersections.

Stetson Kennedy, the author of Jim Crow Guide, offered these simple rules that blacks were suppose to observe in conversing with whites:

1. Never assert or even insinuate that a white person is lying.
2. Never impute dishonorable intentions to a white person.
3. Never suggest that a white person is from an inferior class.
4. Never lay claim to, or overly demonstrate, superior knowledge or intelligence.
5. Never curse a white person.
6. Never laugh derisively at a White person.
7. Never comment upon the appearance of a white female.

When the boundaries of any one of these unspoken laws were violated, there could be serious consequences.

The Freedman's Right to Vote: Poll Taxes

The Poll Taxes was a tax that had to be paid before a person could vote. It was charged to both white and black people. But the tax was started in the 1870's when everyone in the South was still struggling from the recovery from the Civil War. Many freed blacks were still struggling to establish their life in a free society. This tax made it almost impossible for a black person to a vote. This tax also inhibited over 65 percent of the caucasian population from voting.

Literacy Test for Voters

In the 1870's, there was also a literacy test that voters had to pass before they could vote. The education system for freed slaves was still very much in the development stage. The questions asked on the literacy test were fairly uncommon.

For example:

1. Where do presidential electors cast ballots for president?
2. Name the rights a person has after he has been indicted by a grand jury.

This test provided another avenue to deny a freed slave of the right to vote.

"Grandfather Clauses"

The Grandfather clauses were actually laws passed giving some the right to vote if their father or grandfather had been a voting citizen prior to the 15th Amendment being passed. Of course, prior to the 15th Amendment beginning passed, there were only white voters.

Property Ownership

In Alabama up through 1901, a voter had to own at least three hundred dollars worth of property to be given the right to vote. Discrimination and segregation continued to have an enslaving effect on freed people for many more years. But the fight for freedom had not ended.

The Scottsboro Boys

In April 1931, there were nine young black men accused of attacking two white women. The women were of questionable character. Yet, when the black men were accused of attacking them, there was such outcry in the community that Governor Miller had to order the National Guard to protect the suspects.

The case became known as "The Scottsboro Boys Case." This landmark case ended with the young men who were accused eventually being released. The U.S. Supreme Court overturned the convictions because all black jurors in this case were systematically disqualified. It was nineteen years before the last of these young men were released.

Tuskegee Airmen

World War II
99th Squadron

The Tuskegee Airman defied the common racist belief that black men did not have the intellect nor skills to train and serve in the military beside white men as fighter pilots. The segregated Tuskegee Army Air Field School was set up to train black airman. Once a man graduated from the program he would serve in a segregated unit, called "The Red Tail

Angels" flying in more than 200 missions and never losing a plane. By the end of World War II, almost a thousand men had graduated the Tuskegee Air School. These men were the pride of black Americans during the war. They were also proof that black people did have the intelligence to learn anything a white person could learn.

Bus Boycotts

Alabama

At this point in time, when black citizens were still struggling for the right to be treated equally, there was large dependence on public transportation, especially in larger cities of Alabama such as Montgomery and Birmingham. The bus service was used by several thousand passengers each day. Many white (but also a large number of black) citizens used the bus to get to their destination on a daily basis.

The front of the bus was reserved for white passengers, while the black passengers rode in the back of the bus. It was a known 'custom' for black passengers to be expected to stand up if the bus was crowded, allowing white passengers to sit.

Many times, a tired seamstress by the name of Rosa Parks, had given up her seat to a white passenger. But on December 1, 1955, Mrs. Parks refused to stand so a white man could sit. The bus driver told her, if she did not get up and surrender her seat, she would be arrested. Mrs. Parks quietly sat—waiting to be arrested.

Mrs. Parks was quiet but her actions spoke loudly. She had paid the same fare to ride the bus as the white man. Her courage to sit quietly and be arrested, rather than be discriminated against, gave people all over Montgomery and Birmingham the courage to say "no" to the bus. People began to organize rides for one another. They started getting up earlier and walking further. The black citizens refused to ride the public bus system. On February 22, 1956, Rosa Parks, along with others, was arrested again—this time, for helping lead the bus boycotts.

Several of the people in leadership during the bus boycotts had their homes bombed. After more than thirteen months, the bus boycotts were ended with the desegregation of the bus system.

School Desegregation

In May of 1954, after numerous court cases involving segregation had gone before the Supreme Court, the Brown vs. Board of Education case ruled segregation to be unconstitutional. This set in motion the changes that had to be made in a society that had followed the "Separate but Equal" standard for more than twenty years. The freedom fight for Equal Rights had only just begun in Alabama.

In June of 1963, Governor George Wallace stood in the doorway of the University of Alabama, preventing black students from registering for school. President John F. Kennedy called on the Alabama National Guard to remove anyone, including the governor, who blocked the entrance of the school.

Vivian Malone Jones began her college education at the University of Alabama in 1963 and was the first black to graduate from the school in 1965.

Church Bombing in Birmingham

On Sunday, Sept. 15, 1963, at the 16th Street Baptist Church, there was a package placed under the steps of the church. When the bomb contained in the package went off, four little girls were killed while attending their Sunday school class. There were twenty-three others injured in the blast. The church was known as a meeting place for Civil Rights leaders in Alabama.

Alabama Governor, George Wallace, was quoted in the New York Times the week before the church bombing, saying Alabama was going to need a "few first-class funerals" to stop integration. George Wallace fought desegregation for years, but in the last years of his life he openly acknowledged his regret for his behavior and actions toward the black citizens.

CHAPTER 18
SPACE & ROCKET PROGRAM IN ALABAMA

Vocabulary:

Transylvanian
Propelled
Astronomer / Astronomy

Mathematician
Amateur
Chancellor

Hybrid
Petition
Espionage

Research Suggestions:

1. When was the U.S. Space & Rocket Center established?

2. When was Redstone Arsenal established?

3. How many German Scientists actually moved to Huntsville, Alabama to work with the Space Program?

Science & Nature Studies:

Research the space rockets that were designed and built in Huntsville, Alabama.

Timeline

October 28, 1949
Wernher von Braun moves to Huntsville, Alabama.

1951-1955
Gordon Persons is the governor of the state of Alabama.

1953-1961
Dwight D. Eisenhower is President of the United States.

1954
Over a thousand white businessmen meet in Selma, Alabama to organize against school desegregation.

1955
Rosa Parks refuses to give her bus seat up to a white man, beginning the Montgomery Bus Boycott.

1955-1959
James E. Folsom is the governor of the state of Alabama.

1955
City buses in Montgomery were integrated.

Wernher von Braun

Wernher von Braun was born into the German aristocracy on March 23, 1912, during a time of chaos. His father was the Baron Magnus von Braun, a wealthy farmer and minister of agriculture under the Weimar Republic. He had two brothers, Sigsmund one year older and Magnus seven years younger. Wernher was an excellent student in science; however, he had a lack of motivation in the classroom resulting in poor grades. As far as math and physics were concerned, he had no interest and saw no use for them, until he discovered rocketry.

In the 1800's, Francis Scott Key recorded the use of British war rockets when he penned these lines: "the rockets red glare, the bombs bursting in the air." As we all know, these words later became part of the America's beloved national anthem. However, in about 1850, war rockets lost their popularity and were replaced by more powerful weapons of warfare.

In Germany during the 1920's, rocketry was a fad. In the early 20th century, a Russian schoolteacher, Konstantin Tsiolkovsky, revived the interest of rocketry. He perceived that rockets could go where no other form of human transportation could go—outer space.

Also in the 1920's, a Transylvanian mathematician named Hermann Oberth, published a book: Die, Rakete zuden Planetenraumen (The Rocket into Interplanetary Space.) In this publication, he explained the mathematical and physical theory of rocket flight in detail. If you were not scientifically minded it was hard to understand, however, it did include a detailed description of space flight via the rocket. In 1925, this book was discovered by a thirteen-year-old boy named Wernher von Braun. The information contained in this book was absolutely life changing for him! Wernher was already interested and somewhat familiar with rockets. Max Valier, a rocket experimenter, and Fritz von Opel, an automobile maker, built hybrid rocket automobiles propelled by rockets. With these rather fast automobiles, Valier, set record speeds on a track near Berlin. Max Valier was an inspiration to von Braun, and he set out to make his own form of transportation, propelled by rockets of course! He took several rocket fireworks and secured them to a coaster wagon. Then he lit them all at the same time! He later recalled, "I was ecstatic! The wagon was wholly out of control and trailing a comet's tail of fire, but my rockets were performing beyond my wildest dreams." However, the out-of-control wagon was heading straight into Berlin's extremely crowded thoroughfare, the Tiergarten Strasse, and he was arrested. "Fortunately, no one had been injured, so I was released in charge of the Minister of Agriculture, who was my father."

Wernher loved to read science fiction novels by writers such as, Jules Verne and H.G. Wells. He dreamed of the worlds they wrote about. His mother was also an amateur astronomer and for his fourteenth birthday she gave him a telescope. Now he could study the stars and planets! However, Oberth's book brought the two ideas of rocketry and space travel together for von Braun. Now, for the first time, space travel was a reality—not a fantasy. It might actually be possible for humans to go to space! What's more, he saw himself as being the person to build the rockets that would send people into space!

Timeline

1957
Black churches in Montgomery are bombed.

March 28, 1958
W.C. Handy dies at the age 84.

1959-1963
John Patterson is the governor of the state of Alabama.

July 1, 1960
Marshall Space Center is established in Huntsville, Alabama.

1960
Rev. Martin Luther King, Jr. is jailed in Alabama for driving with a Georgia drivers license.

1961
City officials in Birmingham, Alabama vote to close many public areas such as parks and playgrounds rather than integrate them.

1961-1963
John F. Kennedy is President of the United States.

1963-1967
George C. Wallace is the governor of the state of Alabama.

Timeline

1963-1969
Lyndon B. Johnson is President of the United States.

1963
Two black students attempt to enroll at the University of Alabama. Governor George Wallace stands in the entrance to block them from registering. President Kennedy called on the National Guard to remove anyone blocking the doors.

1963
Four young black girls are killed in the Sixteenth Street Baptist Church bombing in Birmingham, Alabama.

1964
Thomas Wesley Martin dies after serving as President of Alabama Power Company for more than 35 years.

1964
Poll taxes are outlawed in federal elections with the passing of 24th Amendment to the Constitution.

When this amazing discovery came to Wernher, he was still thirteen years of age. Forty-four years later, he would send explorers to the moon. Years later, Dr. von Braun described his youthful dreams and desires to a reporter. The following is what he said: "It filled me with a romantic urge. Interplanetary travel! Here was a task worth devoting one's life to! Not just to stare through a telescope at the moon and planets but to soar through the heavens and actually explore the mysterious universe! I knew how Columbus had felt."

It is true Wernher von Braun had a bit of Columbus in him and an extra measure of engineering, too. The two combined equaled a very ambitious young man that would indeed go places and send men to the moon. Due to his poor grades, however, his very angry father sent him to Hermann Lietz Boarding School on Spiekeroog Island in Germany's North Sea. There he discussed his desire to study space travel. Soon after the discussion, he came to an awful realization. He needed to make vast improvements in math and physics, his most dreaded subjects. Well, he did, and within a year he was at the top of his class! Are we not surprised? He was very excited and wanted to further his astronomy studies. Therefore, he went to the principal and persuaded him to purchase a rather expensive telescope for the school. It has been said that this was the training ground for von Braun. Years later, he would petition governments to invest hundreds of thousands of dollars in the research of space and rocket travel. Wernher von Braun excelled so rapidly in his studies at school that his boarding school was willing to allow him to graduate a year in advance.

After graduation, he went to the Charlottenburg Institute of Technology. As part of his education there, he apprenticed at Borsig Works, a machine factory. Here, he found out what being an engineer really meant. His foreman, a gruff, old fashioned man with a mustache and dusty glasses, handed von Braun a chunk of iron and told him to make it into a perfect cube. Wernher later described it as being, "as large as a child's head." When this project reached completion, every side would be smooth, equal, and at right angles with every other face. Von Braun viewed this task as useless. Perturbed, he walked off. Within a few days, he thought he had produced a well "squared" cube. However, much to his disappointment, his foreman disagreed. He started once again, and spent three weeks working on it. Guess what? His foreman rejected it again, the cube was still imperfect! I wonder—was the foreman a perfectionist, or did he just like a job well done?

Maybe he was trying to teach young Wernher a lesson on patience! You know what they say "practice makes perfect!" Then there is that "Patience is a virtue" saying. Von Braun started filing. Here is what he had to say about this particular experience, "Five weeks passed, each day my block grew smaller. My fingers were raw. I was determined to produce a cube he would not reject. Finally I handed him my supreme effort. It was slightly larger than a walnut. Peering over his dusty glasses, he measured every side. My heart pounded. My reward was expressed in one word: "Gut! (Good!)" He had learned a priceless lesson. An engineer must work to exact and precise measurements. Years later, when he built rockets, scientists put their trust in him and the precision of his work.

Timeline

1965
Rev. Martin Luther King Jr. leads marches across Alabama from Selma toward Montgomery in protest of voting rights violations.

1967
Construction of Brown's Ferry begins; at the time it was the world's largest nuclear power plant.

1967-1968
Lurleen B. Wallace is the first female governor of the state of Alabama. She dies while in office.

1967
Alabama is ordered to desegregate its public schools.

1968-1971
Albert P. Brewer is the governor of the state of Alabama.

1968
Rev. Martin Luther King, Jr. is assassinated in Memphis.

1969-1974
Richard M. Nixon is President of the United States.

Timeline

1974-1977
Gerald Ford is President of the United States.

1971-1979
George C. Wallace is the governor of the state of Alabama.

September 25, 1971
Hugo Black dies and is buried in Arlington National Cemetery.

June 5-July 7 1972
Jere Beasley acts as the governor of the state of Alabama.

1972
The Army Corps of Engineers begins work on the largest River Transportation project in the history of the nation. The goal is connecting the Tennessee and Tombigbee Rivers, giving 23 states access to the Mobile Bay.

June 15, 1977
Wernher von Braun dies in Virginia.

1977-1981
Jimmy Carter is President of the United States.

By 1932, German politics were in the same condition they had been in after World War I. To say it plainly—they were in utter turmoil! The worldwide depression did not help either, but instead made politics worse. It was in the year of 1932, when Adolf Hitler was almost elected president of Germany. A year later, Hitler was appointed Chancellor of the Nation of Germany. Shortly afterwards, he seized all power and became full dictator of Germany. We are all very well aware of the many troubles that soon followed. Von Braun did not pay much attention to politics; he was more interested in building rockets. However, the "SS" or the "Protective Squad," Hitler's personal army were, at that point, his employers.

Von Braun and the other scientists were expected to build rockets. However, these rockets were not for space exploration, but rather for killing. They were explosive. Hitler's army wanted to have the capability to destroy enemies at long distances. Von Braun and the other scientists must have thought that someday they would be required to make rockets that would explore outer space. This is what they finally did for the U.S. Government. The first rocket von Braun had planned to build was the Aggregate 1 or the A-1 for short. It was named this because it was formed using an "aggregate" of parts that were undergoing various tests. However, there were some miscalculations and this rocket was never built. The A-2, on the other hand, was built. Two of the A-2 rockets were made and launched successfully. In 1945, von Braun was thirty-three years old. He had been arrested for suspected espionage, nearly killed in a bombing raid, and had built rockets that would fly to outer space. Wow, what an exciting life!

Chapter 18: Space & Rocket Program in Alabama

On May 3, 1945, Wernher von Braun surrendered to American troops. The U.S. Government originally intended to only bring over one hundred scientists. However, one hundred and fifteen German scientists were brought to America. In September of 1945, Wernher von Braun arrived in the United States of America in Boston, Massachusetts, and then went on to Fort Strong, Long Island. After spending two weeks there with six other German scientists and being interrogated, he was shipped to Fort Bliss, Texas. The others were sent to Aberdeen, Maryland. By the early part of 1946, the other scientists had joined him at Fort Bliss. He was very lonely and in early 1947, he married his German cousin, Maria. Wernher brought his new bride and parents back to the U.S. with him. In 1950, the scientists were moved to Redstone Arsenal in Huntsville, Alabama. They were granted U.S. citizenship within two years of moving to Huntsville. The next rocket he built was the "Redstone."

Upon arriving in Huntsville, since this was to be a more permanent job situation, the Germans began to become involved in the social life in Huntsville, Alabama. Their children were enrolled in public schools and they joined community organizations. Of course, there was some uneasiness at first. The people of Huntsville were not sure what to think of Germans that were formally members of the Nazi party living in their city. Moreover, if you have ever moved, you know how the Germans must have felt about living in a new place. In time, these feelings passed and everyone adjusted quite well to the new people, places, and surroundings. The rocket engineers brought a much-needed financial boost to the economy in Huntsville. Because of the rocket engineers who

Timeline

1995-1999
Forrest "Fob" James Jr. is the governor of the state of Alabama.

1980
Jesse Owens dies of lung cancer.

1981-1989
Ronald Reagan is President of the United States.

1983-1987
George C. Wallace is the governor of the state of Alabama.

1985
Tennessee – Tombigbee Waterway opens, connecting 23 states to the Mobile Bay.

1987-1993
Guy Hunt is the governor of the state of Alabama. He was removed from office upon conviction.

1989-1993
George H.W. Bush is President of the United States.

were based in Huntsville, the city became known as the "Rocket City".

On July 16, 1969, Apollo 11 was launched with three astronauts on board: Neil Armstrong, Edwin Aldrin, and Michael Collins. Three days later on July 19, they orbited around the moon and later that day Neil Armstrong became the first man to set foot on the moon. Two hundred and forty thousands miles away, Wernher von Braun watched this historic lunar space landing from his television set, as did the rest of the world. The dream he had since he was thirteen years old finally came true! Some say at the completion of von Braun's dream also came the end of his career. Von Braun retired on June 10, 1972. Five years later, on June 16, 1977, he died in Alexandria, Virginia.

Timeline

1993-1995
James E. Folsom Jr. is the governor of the state of Alabama.

1993
Handy is inducted into Alabama Music Hall of Fame.

1993-2001
William "Bill" Jefferson Clinton is President of the United States.

1999-2003
Don Sigelman is governor of the state of Alabama.

2001-2008
George W. Bush is President of the United States.

October 24, 2005
Rosa Parks dies in her Detroit, Michigan home.

2003-2011
Robert "Bob" Riley is governor of the state of Alabama.

Alabama Counties

County	Date Organized	County Seat
Autauga	November 30, 1818	Prattville
Baine	December 7, 1866	
Baker	December 30, 1868	
Baldwin	December 21, 1809	Bay Minette
Barbour	December 18, 1832	Clayton
Benton	December 18, 1832	
Bibb	February 7, 1818	Centreville
Blount	February 7, 1818	Oneonta
Bullock	December 5, 1866	Union Springs
Butler	December 13, 1819	Greenville
Cahawba	February 7, 1818	
Calhoun	December 18, 1832	Anniston
Chambers	December 18, 1832	Lafayette
Cherokee	January 9, 1836	Centre
Chilton	December 30, 1868	Clanton
Choctaw	December 29, 1847	Butler
Clarke	December 10, 1812	Grove Hill
Clay	December 7, 1866	Ashland
Cleburne	December 6, 1866	Heflin
Coffee	December 29, 184	Elba
Colbert	February 6, 1867	Tuscumbia
Conecuh	February 13, 1818	Evergreen
Coosa	December 18, 1832	Rockford
Cotaco	February 8, 1818	
Covington	December 18, 1821	Andalusia
Crenshaw	November 24, 1866	Luverne
Cullman	January 24, 1877	Cullman
Dale	December 22, 1824	Dale
Dallas	February 9, 1818	Selma
Decatur	December 21, 1821	Commodore
DeKalb	January 9, 1835	Fort Payne
Elmore	February 15, 1866	Wetumpka
Escambia	December 10, 1868	Brewton

Etowah	December 7, 1866	Gadsden
Fayette	December 20, 1824	Fayette
Franklin	February 4, 1818	Russellville
Geneva	December 26, 1868	Geneva
Greene	December 13, 1819	Eutaw
Hale	January 30, 1867	Greensboro
Hancock	February 12, 1850	
Henry	December 13, 1819	Abbeville
Houston	February 9, 1903	Dothan
Jackson	December 13, 1819	Scottsboro
Jefferson	December 13, 1819	Birmingham
Jones	February 4, 1867	
Lamar	February 4, 1867	Vernon
Lauderdale	February 6, 1818	Florence
Lawrence	February 4, 1818	Moulton
Lee	December 15, 1866	Opelika
Limestone	February 6, 1818	Athens
Lowndes	January 20, 1830	Hayneville
Macon	December 18, 1832	Tuskegee
Madison	December 13, 1808	Huntsville
Marengo	February 7, 1818	Linden
Marion	December 13 1818	Hamilton
Marshall	January 9, 1836	Guntersville
Mobile	August 1, 1812	Mobile
Monroe	June 22, 1815	Monroeville
Montgomery	December 6, 1816	Montgomery
Morgan	February 8, 1818	Decatur
Perry	December 13, 1819	Marion
Pickens	December 19, 1820	Carrollton
Pike	December 17, 1821	Troy
Randolph	December 18, 1832	Wedowee
Russell	December 18, 1832	Phenix City
St. Clair	November 20, 1818	Ashville
Sanford	October 8, 1868	
Shelby	February 7, 1817	Columbiana
Sumter	December 18, 1832	Livingston
Talladega	December 18, 1832	Talladega

Tallapoosa	December 18, 1832	Dadeville
Tuscaloosa	February 7, 1818	Tuscaloosa
Walker	December 20, 1824	Jasper
Washington	June 4, 1800	Chatom
Wilcox	December 13, 1819	Camden
Winston	February 12, 1850	Double Springs

Governor Details

Governor / Home County	Dates in Office / Party	Birthplace
William Wyatt Bibb Autauga County	1819-1820 Democrat	Virginia
Thomas Peyton Bibb Limestone County	1820-1821 Democrat	Virginia
Israel Pickens Greene (Hale) County	1821-1825 Democrat	North Carolina
John Murphy Monroe County	1825-1829 Democrat	North Carolina
Gabriel Moore Madison County	1829-1831 Democrat	North Carolina
Samuel B. Moore Jackson County	1831 Democrat	Tennessee
John Gayle Greene (Hale) County	1831-1835 Democrat	South Carolina
Clement Comer Clay Madison County	1835-1837 Democrat	Virginia
Hugh McVay Lauderdale County	1837 Democrat	South Carolina
Arthur Pendleton Bagby Monroe County	1837-1841 Democrat	Virginia
Benjamin Fitzpatrick Autauga County	1841-1845 Democrat	Georgia
Joshua Lanier Martin Limestone County	1845-1847 Democrat	Tennessee

Reuben Chapman .... 1847-1849 .... Virginia
Madison County .... Democrat

Henry Watkins Colllier .... 1849-1853 .... Virginia
Tuscaloosa County .... Democrat

John Anothony Winston .... 1853-1857 .... Alabama
Sumter County .... Democrat
Madison County

Andrew Barry Moore .... 1857-1861 .... South Carolina
Perry County .... Democrat

John Gill Shorter .... 1861-1863 .... Georgia
Barbour County .... Democrat

Thomas Hill Watts .... 1863-1865 .... Alabama
Montgomery County .... Democrat
Butler County

Lewis Eliphalet Parsons .... 1865 .... New York
Talladega County .... Democrat

Robert Miller Patton .... 1865-1867 .... Virginia
Lauderdale County .... Republican

William Hugh Smith .... 1868-1870 .... Georgia
Randolph County .... Republican

Robert Burns Lindsey .... 1870-1872 .... Scotland
Colbert County .... Democrat

David Peter Lewis .... 1872-1874 .... Virginia
Madison County .... Republican

George Smith Houston .... 1874-1878 .... Tennessee
Limestone County .... Democrat

Rufus Wills Cobb .... 1878-1882 .... Alabama
Shelby County .... Democrat
St. Clair County

Edward Asbury O'Neal .... 1882-1886 .... Alabama
Lauderdale County .... Democrat
Madison County

Thomas Seay .... 1886-1890 .... Alabama
Hale County .... Democrat

Thomas Goode Jones .... 1890-1894 .... Georgia
Montgomery County .... Democrat

William Calvin Oates .... 1894-1896 .... Alabama
Henry County .... Democrat
Bullock County

Joseph Forney Johnston .... 1896-1900 .... South Carolina
Jefferson County .... Democrat

William James Samford .... 1900-1901 .... Georgia
Lee County .... Democrat

William Dorsey Jelks .... 1901-1907 .... Alabama
Barbour County .... Democrat
Macon County

Russell McWhorter Cunningham .... 1904-1905 .... Alabama
Jefferson County .... Democrat
Lawrence County

Braxton Bragg Comer .... 1907-1911 .... Alabama
Jefferson County .... Democrat
Barbour County

Emmet O'Neal .... 1911-1915 .... Alabama
Lauderdale County .... Democrat

Charles Hederson .... 1915-1919 .... Alabama
Pike (Bullock) County .... Democrat

Thomas Erby Kilby .... 1919-1923 .... Tennessee
Calhoun County .... Democrat

William Woodward Brandon .... 1923-1927 .... Alabama
Tuscaloosa County .... Democrat
Talladega County

David Bibb Graves .... 1927-1931, 1935-1939 .... Alabama
Montgomery County .... Democrat

Benjamin Meek Miller .... 1931-1935 .... Alabama
Wilcox County .... Democrat

Frank Murray Dixon .... 1939-1943 .... California
Jefferson County .... Democrat

Chauncey M. Sparks .... 1943-1947 .... Alabama
Barbour County .... Democrat

James Elisha Folsom .... 1947-1951, 1955-1959 .... Alabama
Cullman County .... Democrat
Coffee County

Gordon Persons .... 1951-1955 .... Alabama
Montgomery County .... Democrat

John Malcolm Patterson .... 1959-1963 .... Alabama
Russell County .... Democrat
Tallapoosa County

George Corley Wallace .... 1963-1967, 1971-1979, 1983-1987 .... Alabama
Barour County .... Democrat

Lurleen Burns Wallace .... 1967-1968 .... Alabama
Barbour County .... Democrat
Tuscaloosa County

Albert Preston Brewer .... 1968-1971 .... Tennessee
Morgan County .... Democrat

Forrest Hood James .... 1979-1983 .... Alabama
Lee County .... Democrat
Chambers County

Guy Hunt .... 1987-1993 .... Alabama
Cullman County .... Republican

James E. Folsom .... 1993-1995 .... Alabama
Montgomery County .... Democrat

Forrest "Fob" James .... 1995-1999 .... Alabama
Lee County .... Republican

Don Siegelman .... 1999-2003 .... Alabama
Mobile County .... Democrat

Bob Riley .... 2003-2011 .... Alabama
Clay County .... Republican

Kay Ivy .... 2011-Present .... Alabama
Camden County .... Republican

Reading List for *Alabama History in the U.S.*

Life & Times General Sam Dale	J. F. H. Claiborne
Massacre Island	Anne Chancey Dalton
To Kill a Mockingbird	Harper Lee
The Story of My Life	Helen Keller
The Cherokee Hideaway	Wheeler Pounds
Henry Aaron: Dream Chaser	Roz Morris
W.C. Handy: Father of the Blues	Alice Yeager
Emma Sansom: Confederate Heroine	Margie Ross

Additional Recommended Resources

All About Alabama Wildflowers	Jan W. Midgley
Civil War Tales of the Tennessee Valley	Dr. William L McDonald
Lore of the River – The Shoals of Long Ago	Dr. William L McDonald
Chickasaw Chief George Colbert:	Rickey Butch Walker
Doublehead: Last Chickamauga Cherokee Chief	Rickey Butch Walker
Hiking Sipsey: A Family's Fight for Eastern Wilderness	Rickey Butch Walker
Warrior Mountains Folklore	Rickey Butch Walker

BWPublications.com

Published by Bluewater Publications

Bluewater Publications is a multi-faceted publishing company capable of meeting all of your reading and publishing needs. Our two-fold aim is to:

1) Provide the market with educationally enlightening and inspiring research and reading materials.
2) Make the opportunity of being published available to any author and or researcher who so desires to become published.

We are passionate about preserving history and by publishing the research of historians and genealogists, Bluewater Publications is the peoples' choice publisher.

For company information or for information about how you can be published through Bluewater Publications, please visit:

BWPublications.com

Confidently Preserving Our Past,
Angela Broyles
Bluewater Publications

www.ingramcontent.com/pod-product-compliance
Lightning Source LLC
Chambersburg PA
CBHW081848170426
43199CB00018B/2843